A NEWCOMER'S GUIDE TO HAWAII

• • • • • • • • • • • • •

ISLAND WAYS AND CUSTOMS

This book is fondly dedicated to my four "local haoles," Isaac, Jon, Jane, and Judy; to the memory of Ralph and Mike; to a legion of Hawaii friends who left me better than they found me; and to the students who left me wanting to know more.

YOUR SUGGESTIONS?

We'd like your suggestions for *A Newcomer's Guide.* Please send them to Mutual Publishing Co.

LCC 91-067616

Design
Michael Horton Design

First Printing February 1993
1 3 4 5 6 7 8 9

ISBN 0935180-32-X

Mutual Publishing
1127 11th Avenue, Mezz. B
Honolulu, Hawaii 96816
Telephone (808) 732-1709
Fax (808) 734-4094

Printed in Australia

A NEWCOMER'S GUIDE TO HAWAII

ISLAND WAYS AND CUSTOMS

MUTUAL PUBLISHING

BY DAVID PAXMAN
ILLUSTRATED BY CHAD KELIILIKI

ACKNOWLEDGMENTS

Mahalo nui loa to all who helped me gather, check, express, and revise the ideas in this book. Thank you for thinking I could. Thank you, Earl and Audrey Veloria, for the information and even more for your way of being. Thank you, Andrea Sheehan, for your big, loving Hawaiian heart. Thank you, old friends—Bennees, Brueys, Hardistys, Hoods, Grahams, Jacksons, Kamauohas, Pages, Palmers, Porters, Robinsons, Shumways, Smiths, Williamses, and all others from whom I learned island ways. Thanks to all those who thought I was only asking questions from curiosity. Thank you, Hawaii.

TABLE OF CONTENTS

ON DISCOVERING HAWAII

Since Captain James Cook sailed into Hawaiian waters in 1778, millions have learned what it means to discover the Islands. Cook was looking for new lands, life forms, and supply points. He found all of these; more important, he found a people. Since then, hundreds, then thousands, then hundreds of thousands have passed through Hawaii annually. Some came seeking economic opportunity; others came to enjoy the stunning beauty: blue sky and bluer water, lush greenery, yellow sun, and white sand against dark lava mountains. Whatever brought them, and however long their stay, the most successful discoverers had something in common. They realized that it would not be enough to enjoy the mild climate, the world-famous beaches, the little-known scenic wonders, and the delicious island cuisine. Their discovery always meant getting to know the people of Hawaii and adapting to their ways.

Now it's your turn to make discoveries. While time will introduce you to Hawaii's beauties, faces and customs, and the secrets of its racial harmony, this book will help you by giving you the kind of knowledge usually found only among long-term residents.

Information can help only to a point, however. Getting to know Hawaii is also a matter of attitude. A goal of this book is to help you adopt a frame of mind that will lead to satisfying adjustments and good relationships.

Here's to you, Hawaii's latest discoverer.

GETTING ALONG:

ATTITUDES, DO'S AND DON'T'S

EXPECTATIONS AND FANTASIES

A friend confided that after he learned he was being transferred to Hawaii, he would lie awake at night imagining life in the Islands. In his fantasies, Hawaii would be filled with friendly people. Harmonious Polynesian voices would float on the breeze, mixing with the strummed chords of the ***ukulele**** *. He imagined that in the evenings there would be ***lu'aus*** and garden parties, where he would stroll elegantly in his blue yachtsman's blazer and mingle amiably with the beautiful guests. A few local people would quickly become his close friends and introduce him to the secrets of island life. These expectations were created partly by motion pictures and travel advertisements and partly by my friend's desire for a society that filled his inner need for harmony and complete belonging.

Many people have difficulty thinking of the Islands without dreaming of paradise. The problem with such expectations is that they can be true and false at the same time. The simpler and more powerful they are, the more they prevent one from seeing the more complex beauties of island life. These beauties aren't confined to Hawaii's reputation as a fantasy paradise or to its profound natural beauty. They include Hawaii's people as well—neighbors, acquaintances,

*** Words in bold print are discussed in the Alphabetical Guide.**

co-workers, and fellow residents—with their remarkably varied backgrounds, traditions, and ways of getting along.

Previous newcomers can tell how they modified their expectations to match everyday life in Hawaii so that their lives here became richer than the shallow fantasies they began with. Part of the richness comes from the unparalleled friendliness, toleration, and natural beauty, and part comes from the unexpected, and even from the less desirable aspects of day-to-day living. Let's examine how previous newcomers have made the transition.

THE MAINLAND HAOLE IN HAWAII

Not every newcomer is a mainland *haole*, but this group makes up the majority of newcomers. Their experiences are similar to those of many new arrivals. A recent study, *The Mainland Haole: The White Experience in Hawaii*,(1) describes how many *haoles* adjusted to life in the Islands.

The study found that one major factor in the newcomer's adjustment is indeed the tension between expectations and reality. Unlike tourists, who may spend two weeks securely isolated from day-to-day living, the resident newcomer confronts traffic, bugs, and work conditions that wear away the imagery of paradise. Even to consider oneself an "immigrant" is a shock to many *haoles*. Until their move, they've usually been the dominant group, so they see themselves as mainstream and others as ethnic. In Hawaii, Caucasians are just one of many groups and don't necessarily hold the winning cards in education, business, and politics. Consequently, they must learn to found their sense of belonging on something other than being the powerful majority.

Hawaii challenges newcomers to develop new concepts of time and place—and even of their own bodies and skin color. Many people report that after moving to Hawaii, they still found themselves rushing at the old pace, checking items off a list and cramming meetings into a day, yet becoming aware that they were actually losing time in their hyperactive lives. Many newcomers also describe a change in the way they see the landscape. At first they see the land as a scenic attraction and as real estate to be owned and developed; after a few years in Hawaii, they see it as a beautiful and fecund life-giver, a sacred trust which, once "developed," may be lost, or even desecrated.

A final shock for new residents comes when they realize that they symbolize to many locals much of what has gone wrong in Hawaii—too many people, traffic, commercialization, and the loss of island culture.

Frictions and stresses of daily life exist in Hawaii as elsewhere. But, because newcomers find themselves in a new setting and sense their difference from the island people, they may erroneously perceive the frictions as personal affronts. Often, a period of disillusionment follows their initial enthusiasm. Then their enthusiasm returns, but much changed. They have learned how other people think and feel, so they now take part in island life as long-term citizens, not short-term spectators.

SOME SUGGESTIONS

How do you adjust to the differences, the multifaceted acceptance and alienation, and the competing interests that make up modern Hawaii? How do you do this and remain alive to the astounding beauty of life and the unparalleled spirit of *aloha* and cooperation that sets Hawaii apart from other mixed societies around the globe?

A neighbor who has resided in Hawaii most of his life answered this way: "You get along here when you go beyond putting up with differences, and even beyond accepting them, and you actually start valuing them. Sometimes the closest you can get to people with different backgrounds and traditions is to glimpse how very different you are without wishing to make them like yourself."

Which leads to the other side of differences: human similarities. The same qualities that create friendship and cooperation anywhere also apply here. One key to getting along is to convey the same attitudes to others that you wish them to extend to you. If this all sounds like a mini-course in human relations, you've got the point. Treat people as if they mattered just as much as you do. This does not mean dripping with emotion or being overeager. It does mean attending to simple things, such as how well you listen, how you respond when asked to bring food to a party or game (your response will often be more carefully observed than you think), how you assume the best when you could interpret things negatively, and so forth. And don't be surprised to find that many locals are cautious and guarded toward those not of their own background. When you sense these attitudes, remember that history has given them good reason to feel this way.

WHAT IS "LOCAL"?

Hawaii residents often distinguish between "locals" and "outsiders." What does it mean to be "local"? One author has written:

> Those that say they are "local" are saying that they distinguish themselves from people who they believe are not sensitive to the racial and cultural forces operating in Hawaii. It means that they share a special language, a special mode of behavior, a special value system, and a special racial experi-

ence which separates them and other "locals" from the "outsiders." As "locals" they believe that they respect the diversity of people around them while also appreciating their commonness of lifestyles and attitudes.(2)

Local people do not see themselves as "natives" and do not like being called that, or hearing innuendos that mean the same thing. They are proud of their identities and sensitive to negative comments, even when indirect, ignorant, or well-intended. For instance, almost all newcomers at some point have the urge to enlighten their local friends and neighbors as to how something is done on the mainland. This may happen at a PTA meeting, a community association meeting, or a more casual gathering. Often, newcomers expect to impress others by sharing their wisdom with the local people. But the effect is just the opposite. The newcomers look as if they think they are superior. Does this mean that you can't make suggestions? No. But find a way that doesn't make you look good at the expense of others. Keep in mind, too, that if you open your eyes you'll find countless ways of doing things here in the Islands that could benefit others. Not the least of these is our tolerance, patience, and willingness to accept others the way they are and to find solutions that are mutually satisfying.

Local people appreciate newcomers who adapt to their ways and, to some extent, they expect this as the price of getting along.

Here, for example, are the comments of two Hawaiian friends, both of whom were born and grew up in Hawaii, graduated from college, and lived several years on the mainland before returning permanently to the Islands. When asked, "What would you tell newcomers about getting along in Hawaii?" one responded:

> When new people come from the mainland, they want to get involved in the community, but at the meetings they state their views aggressively, the way they've learned to. They don't understand how the local people think on some issues. But they speak their minds, not like the locals do. So sometimes it almost winds up physical.
>
> A newcomer needs to practice a little restraint in the way he speaks if he wants to fit in. Otherwise, he may get his way, but the locals will close up and not have anything to do with him.
>
> We have some *haole* teachers out here that have been here a long time—longer than me in this place. They're used to hearing our kids vent their feelings against certain groups (mostly *haoles*), so they know how the local people feel, but they get over that and stay around. People know they're not just here for a short time to buy real estate. They know how to blend in, know how to walk into a *lu'au* without attracting attention or sending messages, "I'm from outside."

Another friend, a woman, said this:

> When they come here, people need to change their idea of time. They should slow down a bit, not always be rushing through things. Also, they should not always assume a bad judgment if they have a run-in with local people. You really need to be aware of local history and politics to know why local people react the way they do. People shouldn't draw conclusions that someone doesn't like them if they seem unfriendly at first. Sometimes it carries over from earlier times when the haole was always the boss and the Hawaiian or immigrant was the laborer. The white man was *luna* [supervisor, foreman]. A lot of resentment was built up.
>
> Around here, everything used to be plantation. When they shut down the plantation, lots of people lost jobs. Now they are

slowly developing the land, but local people can't afford it. They worked it, but only outsiders with money can afford to move in. Local people see this and it gives them a bad taste for the people who do move in and buy.

This doesn't mean locals automatically don't like newcomers, but sometimes they seem unfriendly at first to see what the reaction will be. In the locals, the heart is always there, but it just needs to be reached first.

Even local people can get tested like this. When I taught on one part of the island, kids and parents were hard on me at first. I'm part Hawaiian and thought I would get along real easy. They wanted to know who I thought I was, coming with a college degree and nice clothes to tell them how to live. Did I think I was better than them, or what? I had to spend a lot of time with the kids, make home visits and play with the chickens and such to break down the barriers.

DO'S AND DON'T'S

DO take a gift with you when you visit someone. No need for something grand or impressive. A little food will do. Observing this local tradition will mark you as a caring and sharing person.

DO observe people around you. Without staring or being conspicuous, watch people interact to get a sense of their ways and rhythms of life.

DO slow down a bit. Be patient in explaining what you want from others and in listening to their response. Try not to communicate that you and your objectives are more important than they are.

DO be actively friendly. Greet others in a friendly, polite way, even if they don't greet you.

DO offer to share things: food, time, tools, expertise.

DO join local service and social organizations: scouting, band booster groups, neighborhood associations, civic clubs, auxiliaries, and so forth.

DO take the initiative in inviting people to your place or sending food over to theirs.

DO be yourself.

DO relax.

DON'T be overeager. Don't glad-hand everyone in sight. Don't act like you've got to master all local customs by sundown. Instead, make a friend first and let your friend show you what he or she considers important.

DON'T show off. Most local people detest arrogance and loudness in newcomers. Assuming that you learn from this book, show how much you have learned by not parading it.

DON'T start thinking that the Islands are on trial. A person who has been offended may unconsciously begin judging everyone and everything around, and usually with a "guilty" verdict. It's much wiser initially to consider yourself on trial.

DON'T assume you have to speak pidgin to get along. Most newcomers that try their pidgin wings sound foolish. Locals think of pidgin as their insider language. They are flattered but embarrassed when newcomers ape local speech to fit in.

DON'T try to change the people of Hawaii. If you have something to teach them, let it come through your actions, not your mouth.

DON'T look for fights. If you are young and male, don't get in a staring match with a local guy. Guaranteed, the staring won't last very long. Local young men take deliberate eye-to-eye contact as a challenge unless you know them or are already talking.

DON'T honk in traffic when you get impatient or want to play cop. Use your horn for danger.

FOR A FAST START

To get a quick overview of the most important island ways, read the following sections in the **Alphabetical Guide:**

'Aina
Aloha
Food
Lei
Malihini
Pidgin
Shaka
Shoes
Talk Story

KIDS AND SCHOOLS

KIDS AND SCHOOLS

No matter how far you've moved in miles or lifestyle, your children will judge your Hawaii relocation by their success in making new friends. As parents, you're no doubt equally concerned with their placement and success in school.

QUALITY OF SCHOOLS

How good are the schools? It depends on what you mean by good and which schools you mean. For a complete answer, you must take into account the social and academic components of education, differences in academic achievement among public schools, and differences between public and private schools.

Standardized test scores provide the quickest reading of the quality of Hawaii's schools, but tests can't measure the true strengths of Hawaii public education. These are social. Attending school with children of remarkably varied backgrounds can open a young mind as no class in intercultural relations can ever do. Even the social tensions that naturally result from the proximity of so many different students can be like so many personal tutors.

Children who are accustomed to belonging to the majority are often shocked when they move to Hawaii to find themselves merely a member of one of many racial and ethnic groups. The smug self-assurance of those who have grown up dominating others socially and economically may fall as a casualty of Hawaii education. On the other hand, children accustomed to being in a minority can find Hawaii a welcome change because they have so much company: nearly everyone is minority. Hawaii education is strong on toleration, cooperation, group identity across differences, and preservation of the Islands' history and cultures.

On the more easily measured side of academics, Hawaii public education scores just below national averages but is improving. This educational lag must be viewed in context. Hawaii is still overcoming a heritage in which public schools served questionable political ends and perpetuated, not alleviated, inequities between races. Consider the English Standard School System, launched in 1924 and lasting until

1947. It established higher admissions standards and more uniform instruction at designated high schools. Since admission hinged on a young person's English language ability, however, the system helped segregate Caucasians and the most educated of the other racial groups from the rest of a dark-skinned, undereducated population.

Hawaii is the only state in the Union that runs public education through a unified, state-wide school system. This system is partly the legacy of Hawaii's days as a Territory, but it has another rationale. The state-wide system ensures that funding, facilities, staffing, and opportunities are kept roughly on par, whether a student lives on the tip of Molokai or at the top of a high-rise in Honolulu. If public education were turned over to districts, as on the mainland, the differences in funding and achievement would be even wider than they are now. The trade-off for uniform funding, however, is a heavy layer of administration that hinders flexibility and initiative.

With the advent of democratic policies, state-controlled planning, and greater funding, the more unfortunate traits of Hawaii education are disappearing, but the system still struggles with a rigid bureaucracy, poor classroom discipline, social tensions, and vandalism. Perhaps its most difficult challenge is the task of motivating and instructing a diverse student population, many of whose families do not have strong English-language skills or traditions of education. Still, test scores over the last decade have shown modest, but steady, improvement. In 1978, 34% of Hawaii's tenth-graders scored below average. In 1989, only 22% scored below average.

These scores provide a quick way of ascertaining the quality of public education, but one must interpret them cautiously. Most

educators believe that the tests can assess changes over time and draw attention to the differences within the state system much better than reveal differences between Hawaii and the mainland. Keeping in mind these cautions, let's examine test scores more closely to see what they reveal.

Hawaii's primary schools score from slightly above, to well below, the national average. Overall, though, Hawaii's children achieve at about the same levels as their peers on the mainland. The following graph compares the 1990 national third- and sixth-grade averages in reading and math with those of Hawaii.

ELEMENTARY SCHOOLS—STATE AVERAGES

	Below average	Average	Above average
U.S. Total	23%	54%	23%
Hawaii math			
3rd grade	19	49	32
6th grade	20	45	35
Hawaii reading			
3rd grade	24	58	18
6th grade	22	57	21

The next chart compares tenth-grade students with those of the nation. Notice that in reading, tenth-graders have slipped down from the standings held by elementary-schoolers.

TENTH-GRADE SCORES—STATE AVERAGES

	Below average	Average	Above average
U. S. Total	23%	54%	23%
Hawaii math	21	49	30
Hawaii reading	23	61	16

As the figures make clear, high-school scores are further below national levels than are those of primary schools. What mysterious factor causes Hawaii to fall behind after grade six? One reason:

a fairly large number of above-average students depart public to attend private schools in junior high and high school. Their absence effectively lowers the average scores for public schools. But that does not seem to explain everything. The learning environment seems to weaken in many high schools, as young teens test their power in a permissive society and as teachers lose the kind of control typical in elementary schools. Another dimension: high schools in affluent areas, where parents emphasize education and support academic achievement, score consistently higher than those in poorer areas. With these facts in mind, we can survey the 1990 tenth-grade test scores.

TENTH-GRADE SCORES BY SCHOOL

READING:	below/average/above			MATH: below/average/above		
U.S. Totals	23%	54%	23%	23%	54%	23%
HONOLULU DISTRICT						
Farrington	41	54	5	22	59	19
Kaimuki	27	56	17	20	47	33
Kaiser	12	70	19	13	52	36
Kalani	18	58	24	8	37	55
McKinley	16	64	20	10	44	46
Roosevelt	17	62	21	15	40	45
CENTRAL DISTRICT						
Aiea	20	62	18	18	47	35
Leilehua	26	57	17	24	47	29
Mililani	8	64	28	9	47	43
Moanalua	14	60	26	10	46	44
Radford	20	59	20	19	57	24
Waialua	28	63	9	25	58	17
LEEWARD DISTRICT						
Campbell	28	63	9	24	57	18
Nanakuli	49	49	2	41	52	7

Pearl City	14	65	21	17	40	43
Waianae	39	55	6	36	54	10
Waipahu	31	59	9	21	53	26
WINDWARD DISTRICT						
Castle	21	64	15	22	47	31
Kahuku	23	62	15	32	50	18
Kailua	24	61	15	17	51	32
Kalaheo	14	66	20	18	50	32
NEIGHBOR ISLAND—AVERAGES ONLY						
Big Island	24	59	17	27	49	24
Maui	24	61	15	22	52	26
Kauai	25	60	15	24	55	21

PUBLIC OR PRIVATE?

If you are considering private schools for your children, you'll be pleased to know that Hawaii has excellent private schools. But, before you look for a private school, be aware of the ways that public schools are devoting their best teachers and more resources to advanced students. Students in these programs receive greater intellectual challenge, artistic guidance, talent development, recognition, and even college credit.

Gifted and Talented programs exist in nearly all schools in the Islands. Students are selected by teacher recommendation and test scores, but parental requests can also be considered. Programs vary from school to school, so visit the school administration or program heads to learn which subjects and talent areas they offer.

Advanced Placement programs exist in nearly all island high schools. Classes are taught by selected teachers to motivated students capable of mastering subjects with greater depth and speed. In most subjects, students may earn college credit by taking special examinations.

Most high schools also offer English, math, history, and science classes at various levels within each grade so that students can learn among peers of similar abilities. When you enroll your children, make sure to inquire about opportunities to place them in learning situations matched to their abilities.

Through the Learning Center program, each high school develops resources and expertise in a particular field, such as science, music, performing arts, business, media communications, and so on. The Learning Center program in your area's high school makes it possible for your child to take more specialized, varied, and advanced classes in that special field. Be sure to ask which program your school offers.

My family's experience may be illuminating. We chose public schools, even though the high school serving our area was, at the time, well below average, even for Hawaii. By helping our children choose their teachers, working with school counselors on placement and schedules, taking advantage of accelerated and Advanced Placement classes, and working quietly to support academic improvement, we helped our children receive the best their schools could offer. We felt proud of their schools and confident of the quality of their education.

A directory listing schools, personnel, and calendars is available for $3.00 from the State Department of Education, Communications Branch, P.O. Box 2360, Honolulu, HI 96804.

PRIVATE SCHOOLS

For every six students in public schools, Hawaii has one attending private schools, the highest proportion in the nation. Why? First of all, private education took off from a strong start. Many private schools originated before an adequate public system was available and when children of the elite were segregated from the general school-age population. Punahou School, for example, was founded in 1841.

But this alone doesn't entirely explain the present strength of private schools. To remain in their current robust condition, private schools offer something very different from elitism and segregation, although they are sometimes accused of perpetuating these. Some schools offer special emphases and learning environments; some offer boarding arrangements; some offer close supervision and counseling for troubled youth; some offer an academic excellence many families are willing to pay for when they don't find it in public schools; and certain schools offer religious instruction unavailable in public schools.

Private schools differ in size, emphasis, and tuition. Some stress academic preparation for higher education; others, creativity and balance; and others, basic skills for students with learning disabilities.

Here are brief facts on the larger private schools offering high school diplomas.

School	**Size**	**Tuition** (92-93)	**Comment**
Damien	435	$ 3,950	Catholic. Boys only. College-oriented, traditional curriculum. 12 sports.
Hawaii Baptist Academy	500	$ 5,720	Baptist. Coed. College-oriented curriculum.
Hawaii Prep. Academy	200	$15,800	Coed boarding school on Big Island. Residential. Stresses balance, self-esteem.
Iolani	1,700	$ 6,600	Episcopal. Coed, formerly boys only. Academic excellence, college preparation. 17 sports.
Kamehameha	2,400	$ 1,220	Protestant. Funded by the Bishop Estate for nondenom. students of Hawaiian ancestry. College prep., strong in performing arts.

Maryknoll	500	$4,600	Catholic. Coed. College prep. and personal development.
Mid-Pacific	1,000	$6,525	Coed. Boarding tuition $10,125. Christian orientation.
Punahou	3700	$7,150 (K-12)	Christian. Coed. Academic excellence, innovative curriculum. Strong in sports. Considered the best in Hawaii.
Sacred Hearts	976	$4,200 (K-12)	Catholic. Girls. College prep. and personal development.
St. Andrew's Priory	650	$6,000	Episcopal. Girls. College prep., values, sports.
St. Anthony	425	$3,100	Catholic. Coed. Basic skills, music, and art. On Maui.
St. Francis	300	$3,500	Catholic. Girls. Personalized educ. with college prep. curriculum.
St. Louis	850	$4,410	Catholic. Boys. Accelerated, general and developmental programs. Balance of spiritual, intellectual, physical.

If you are considering independent schools, you can obtain the current *Directory of the Hawaii Association of Independent Schools* by writing to 2445 Kaala St., Honolulu, HI 96822.

GETTING ALONG AT SCHOOL

Elementary school children, more accepting than their elders, seem to adjust more easily than those in high school. In either case, making new friends will depend on many factors: a child's shyness, the children in the immediate neighborhood, and luck. If you feel concerned about your elementary school child's adjustment, consider the following:

1. If you know families with children of the same age as yours, arrange through their parents to have them walk to school and play together.
2. Take the initiative: ask your child which others in the class he or she likes, and arrange for them to play at your house after school. Be sure to include a treat and fun things to do.
3. Bring to school treats for the whole class. Let the teacher know ahead, of course.
4. Approach the teacher about your child's adjustment.Ask advice.
5. Be your child's friend. Arrange after-school outings and games, and be alert for chances to invite other kids along.
6. Remember that adjustments can be difficult anywhere. Children from Hawaii who move to the mainland also have difficulty feeling accepted.
7. Don't interfere too much. Be patient; children are remark-

ably resilient. Sometimes it's a mistake to take control of their lives.

8. Whether or not your child feels immediately at home, get involved in his or her school. Doing so will also help you adjust, belong, and contribute to your new community. Join the PTA, volunteer as a room mother or dad, help with the school pageant or carnival, or offer to teach a special skill in your child's classroom.

In junior high and high school, newcomers may fit in immediately or may be tested and teased. Students at these levels, whether locals or newcomers, tend to be more socially aware and cautious. Young people, asked to give advice on how newcomers can adjust, give the same message: newcomers should blend in and should especially avoid snobbish or obnoxious behavior. As a general rule, local kids detest newcomers who are loudmouths or show-offs. Local students are aware that newcomers are sizing them up, just as they are sizing up the newcomers. If they sense that newcomers look down on them, it will be doubly hard for them to extend acceptance and friendship. The situation calls for open minds and patience. Local students generally see themselves as willing to make friends. A newcomer is best advised to make a friend or two and then ask advice on other points that come up.

Aside from discussing the local viewpoint with your children, here are suggestions on how to help secondary school children get in the flow:

1. Help your children be alert for other newcomers and treat them as friends. They will be going through the same adjustments.
2. Help your children join a club or school organization. Be longing to a band, working on the school paper, or helping organize a dance can help young people feel they belong and form friendships. A school counselor can suggest groups and activities.
3. Use your contacts at work, or in church or civic organizations, to steer your children to others with whom they might become friends.

4. Help your children understand that many local people do not respond favorably to newcomers who try to make a big splash or impress others. Their first few weeks in a new school are a time to find a small number of friends and to get the rhythm and flow of school life, not to show off how much one knows or steal someone's boyfriend or girlfriend. A little restraint in giving right answers to teachers' questions may also be in order.
5. Hawaii is very sports conscious. Athletic ability in any sport can be a great asset in making a place for oneself. Football and basketball dominate, but other sports should not be overlooked. Volleyball is very popular. Track, tennis, golf, surfing, wrestling, and soccer teams often have room for new players, even if their skill levels are not that high.
6. As a parent, take part in school. The more you attend meetings, help with extracurricular programs, and so forth, the more aware you will be of school conditions and the more comfortable you will feel helping to improve them.
7. Prepare your kids not to be offended by labels such as "*haole.*" As often as not, these are used with neutral, or even friendly, overtones.

DRESS AT SCHOOL

Except at private schools with dress codes or uniforms, school kids dress very casually. In elementary school, many even go barefoot; most wear slippers (flip-flops). Shorts, jeans, and T-shirts abound. Girls who wear skirts or dresses usually wear shorts over their underwear so they can play games or swing on the jungle-gym modestly.

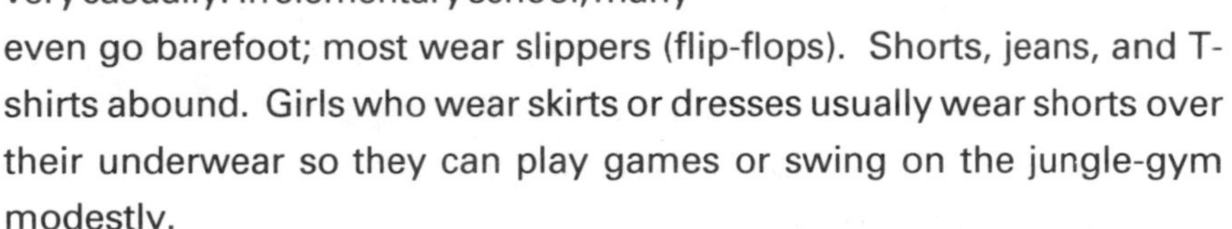

In secondary schools, dress continues casual, though one rarely will see anyone barefoot.Girls wear shorts, jeans, slacks, or skirts with T-shirts, blouses, or even sweat-shirts and sweaters on cool days. Boys dress in much the same style: shorts, jeans, or casual slacks with T-shirts or sport shirts.

PIDGIN

Pidgin—formally known as Hawaii Creole English—is a permanent feature of island life. Among local children, it is the medium of communication around the playground, playing field, and neighborhood. Understanding this dialect can be an important step in fitting in. However, most local children don't expect newcomers to be fluent in pidgin as a condition for acceptance. If anything, they are irritated when outsiders try to imitate their lingo. Until one has been here a long time, the use of a few of the most common words and phrases will be enough to help one fit in.

When your children do begin to master pidgin, show interest and encouragement. Don't worry that their English will deteriorate. They are capable of operating in both languages and will generally have a keen sense of when each is appropriate.

For further information on this rich variety of language, see the section on pidgin in the alphabetical guide and consult **Pidgin You Should Know** in the **Glossaries.**

DATING

You may find that dating practices in high school differ from those where you come from. For example, in some schools, it is not customary to date several different girls or guys at a time. Rather, a girl and guy "go together," as soon as they start to show interest in each other, even though they don't know each other well and have barely dated in the evening. This custom can be quite a shock to a newcomer who finds that a friendship at school is interpreted by others as a commitment. Because of this custom, boy-girl relationships in some high schools can seem a little possessive. Your children should ask their local friends for advice on how to treat their friendships until they develop their own sense of what goes and what doesn't.

PEOPLES, VALUES, LIFESTYLES OF HAWAII

At a recent college graduation on Oahu, a young woman from Singapore remarked, "Hawaii is a melting pot, just like my home." Then she added: "But here people melt faster."

Hundreds of thousands of newcomers have "melted faster" into Hawaii's people. However, each group that makes up Hawaii's population has also resisted disappearing completely by holding onto the traditions that made them distinct to begin with. At first, immigrants clustered together in plantation villages, preserving their languages and customs because they planned to return to their native lands. After they realized that Hawaii had become their permanent home, they wanted assimilation more than segregation. Finally, when their economic and legal status was secure, they realized that their assimilation threatened to make them culturally indistinguishable. At this point, they reached back to revive the language, customs, festivals, and arts of their ancestors.

Hawaii culture is therefore made up of many commonly shared customs and attitudes that are called "local," while it is also a combination of the distinct ways of each group. Knowing island ways means knowing each major group and recognizing their contributions to local customs. This section glances at the history, traditions, and values of Hawaiians and the major immigrant groups in the order of their arrival.

HAWAIIANS

History. No matter how powerful immigrant peoples have become politically and economically, and no matter how many times and in how many ways the Hawaiians have had to make room for

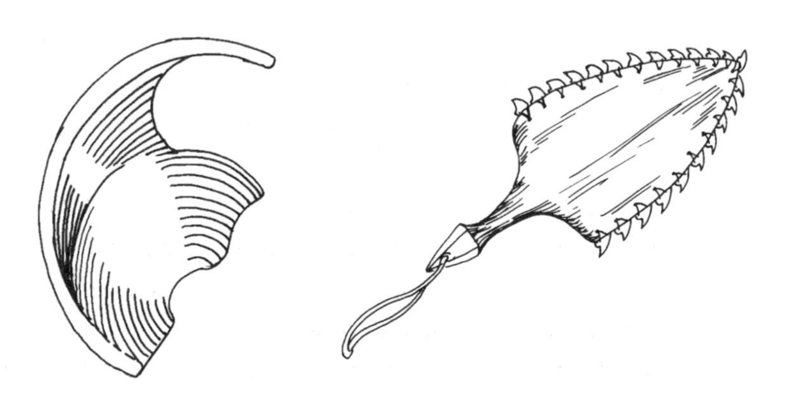

others, Hawaiian culture is still the dominant force in island life. Part of this influence reflects the lasting recognition that the Islands belong to the Hawaiian people in a way not true for any other group; part reflects the many attractive features of Hawaiian culture. The spirit of ***aloha***, the melodious Hawaiian language, the ***'ohana*** view of family

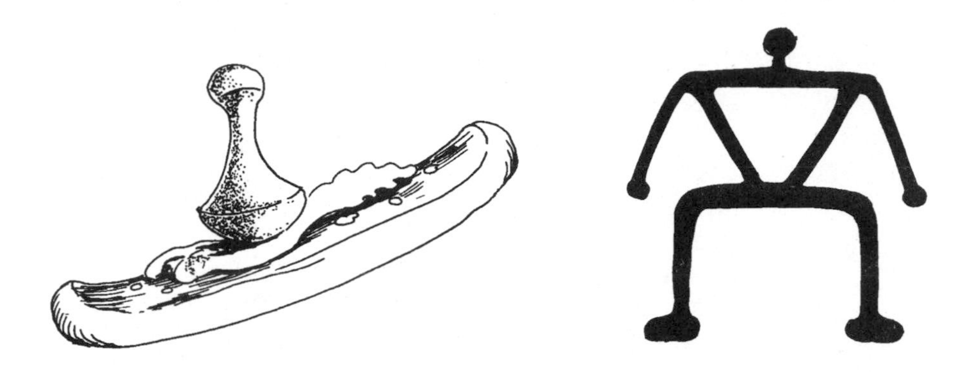

relations, the qualities of generosity and loyalty, the ***lu'au's*** celebration of food and friends, the flower lei, the assertive ancient and the graceful modern ***hula***—all these and many other customs maintain the special appeal of Hawaiian culture.

Historians have formed two major theories to explain how the Polynesians arrived in Hawaii. Some believe that they came originally from Southeast Asia and slowly migrated into the Pacific, with Hawaii being one of their last settlements. Others believe that they came from South America, drifting on currents across the Pacific from east to west.

Both theories have supporting evidence. Blood-type studies show that Polynesians may have links with the Indian peoples of Central and South America. The same strain of sweet potato is found in Hawaii and South America, and in both places it has nearly the same name (*kumala* in South America; *'uala* in Hawaii). But New-World evidences are open to some doubt. Similar blood types can be found in distant peoples with no possible connections, and the sweet potato could as easily have traveled east as west.

Evidence for the Southeast Asia migration theory is stronger.

Many Polynesian words have cognates (linguistic cousins) in Southeast Asian languages such as Malay. Studies of Lapita pottery (a kind of earthenware vessel found in the South Pacific and Southeast Asia) suggest similar techniques and designs. Third, some Polynesian tools seem to have Asian origins. Obviously, some combination of the two migrations may possibly have occurred.

Whatever route the early Polynesians took, they probably arrived from Tahiti beginning around 900 A.D. (some scholars date the first settlements as early as 200 A.D.). Language, legends, physical features of the people, building styles, and artifacts, such as tools and fishhooks, clearly point to Tahiti as the home of Hawaii's first settlers. The early Polynesian settlers developed a complex but unified way of life with a class structure of royalty, *ali'i* or nobles, and *maka'ainana* or commoners; a set of *kapu* or strict taboos governing all facets of daily life and social interaction; a rich heritage of myths, legends, and poetic chants; a close relationship with the *'aina* or land, and all forms of life; a system of land division into *ahupua'a* or districts running from shore to mountains; a calendar of ordinary life and *makahiki* or celebration; classes of *kahuna* or priests and craftsmen; and a religion that was not a separate activity as in most other cultures, but an integral part of every aspect of life.

When Captain Cook and his sailors anchored off Waimea, Kauai, on Cook's third voyage to the Pacific, they found a thriving people, estimated at 300,000 total, fishing the shorelines and farming the coastal plains and valleys. If 1778 opened Hawaii to outside influence, the next few decades were equally momentous in Hawaiian political history. In that time, the Hawaiian Islands were united for the first time under a single ruler, King Kamehameha of the Big Island.

These two events, discovery and political unification, contained the seeds of a radically new future: the establishment of Hawaii as a stopping-off place for ships; a sharp decline in population as Western diseases ravaged the Hawaiian people; the arrival of Christian missionaries in 1820; the political rule of the Hawaiian monarchy; the growth of the sugar industry and the consequent importation of tens of thousands of workers; the eventual overthrow of Queen Lili'uokalani in 1893; the annexation of the Islands by the United States in 1898; and statehood in 1959. Through all these changes, the Hawaiian people have undergone painful transitions. Where they once ruled, they are now largely ruled. Where they were the sole indigenous population, they are now a minority. Where they were possessors, they are now largely dispossessed.

Today, pure Hawaiians number less than 10,000. They and the much larger group of part-Hawaiians (120,000 to 180,000, depending on how you count) comprise only about an eighth of the population. In spite of their relative population decline, however, their political, cultural, and economic powers have increased in the last two decades. A Hawaiian Renaissance has united this people in the desire to retain their culture, language, and values. Hawaiian activists are using legal, political, and mass-media means to retain and regain legal rights, recognition, and redress. Several groups are pushing for a Native Hawaiian Nation, similar in legal status to that of American Indian tribes on the mainland. Others press for compensation for the loss of lands and economic power. Regardless of the outcome of these issues, residents owe homage to the Hawaiians for their extraordinary cultural heritage.

Values and Traditions. A group of cultural leaders identified at least twenty-five attributes important in Hawaiian culture. These included *aloha*, humility, generosity, hospitality, spirituality, cooperativeness, graciousness, industry, patience, competitiveness, intelligence, and helpfulness. It should be obvious from this list that Hawaiian values are diverse. In a summary way, they can be conveyed, though incompletely, in the following terms, each of which is more fully defined in the alphabetical portion of the guide:

Aloha: the spirit of love and welcome

'Aina: the land as life-giver and nurturer

'Ohana: the extended family, with its obligations of loyalty, cooperation, and respect for elders

Lu'au: the feast, a celebration of the abundance of life through food and the gathering together of people

Hula: dance with accompanying chants or songs

A number of state holidays commemorate the Hawaiian heritage: **Kamehameha Day** (June 11) honors the great monarch who ruled from 1795 to 1819. **Kuhio Day** (March 26) honors Prince Kuhio, the second Hawaii delegate to Congress.

Lei Day (May 1) is not a state holiday, but celebrates the Hawaiian heritage through the lei. A number of *hula* festivals feature ancient and modern forms of that dance.

CAUCASIANS

Since most readers have ample awareness of the *haole* or Caucasian lifestyle, little will be said about it here. But we can't move on without noting that the Caucasians were the first outside group to enter Hawaii and that their imprint on Hawaiian affairs can hardly be overstated. After Captain Cook and his mariners arrived in 1778, news of the Islands quickly spread among sea-going nations. Hawaii became an important station in trans-Pacific voyages and whaling. Then came deserting sailors, Christian missionaries from New England in 1820, merchants, planters, and professionals, as well as vagabonds and opportunists. Hawaiian monarchs retained advisors and appointed ministers from among the white population, and an export economy grew under the initiative of white organizers and investors. In the 1890s, a white population with strong ties to the United States helped overthrow the monarchy and cede the Islands to the United States. In the twentieth century, a large number of Caucasians have come with the military. Beginning in the 1960s, a wave of young people comprised of hippies, surfers, and entrepreneurs has had wide influence.

Caucasians are now the single largest immigrant group in Hawaii, having recently overtaken the Japanese in that role. They have exerted leadership in all aspects of public and private life: politics, business, the arts, education, religion, defense, etc. The same qualities that drove them to leadership are also at the heart of their somewhat ambivalent stereotype. *Haoles* are known for their ambition, hard work, curiosity, inventiveness, education, and intellect, as well as for their loudness, materialism, self-interest, and coldness.

CHINESE

History. The Chinese were the first outside group brought in to provide labor for the growing sugar industry. Between 1852 and 1898, about 50,000 immigrants came from Southern China. A typical contract bound workers to a six-day workweek for five years. In return, they would get free passage to Hawaii and receive wages of $2 per month, plus housing, food, and medical care. Most immigrants were men who planned on saving enough to return to China. About half did return, but those who stayed often left the plantation at the end of their contract period. Many married Hawaiian women or arranged for Chinese brides to be sent to Hawaii. By 1883, the Chinese made up nearly a fourth of the island population, leading to fears that they might become too unified both on and off the plantations. The government restricted further immigration, and plantation owners looked to the Portuguese Madeira Islands and Japan to diversify the labor force so it could be more easily controlled.

Once off the plantation, the Chinese turned to farming, trades, and small business and began to advance up the economic and social ladder. As their prosperity allowed them to buy homes in more

exclusive neighborhoods, their alliances with other less prosperous races and groups allowed them to gain political power. Their emphasis on education, family, work, and owning property accelerated their rise in status. A study of the Chinese found that within two generations of 1890, six out of ten Chinese entered careers in the professions (especially medicine), ownership of businesses, clerical work, or skilled trades. During World War II, they consolidated their power bases in politics and business management that they created before the war years. Today, the Chinese wield influence far beyond what one would expect of a small minority of only six percent of the total population.

Values and Traditions. When asked what it was like to grow up Chinese in Hawaii, a Chinese professional man laughingly responded, "guilt." He then went on to explain important qualities of Chinese culture that make it stand apart from today's American ways: respect for parents and elders, a strong motivation to succeed not just for oneself, but to improve the immediate family's welfare and security, and an emphasis not on individual feeling and desire but on proper behavior as defined by the rules and traditions of Chinese culture.

Many traditional traits of Chinese families are disappearing in Hawaii today. Arranged marriages, the subordination of the female to the male, and the subordination of a new wife to her mother-in-law are rare now. But, even with the inevitable loosening of the older, traditional family patterns, Chinese families continue to instill attitudes of hard work at school and on the job, responsibility for the success of the family, and respect for one's elders. The stereotype of the inscrutable, polite Chinese, though misleading, has grown out of the tendency of the Chinese to channel strong feeling into socially acceptable manifestations.

Some traditions of the Chinese are:

Chinese medicine, based on harmony of the organs and use of medicinal foods and herbs.

Chinese New Year, occurring in January or February each year.

Crack seed, various kinds of prepared seeds and fruit.

Ching Ming, a festival on April 5, when Chinese honor their dead by placing food offerings near their grave sites.

Fireworks, set off on special occasions to frighten away evil spirits.

Li-see or red money, money wrapped in red paper and given on special occasions to convey good wishes and good luck.

Lion dance, a team dance using a large lion costume symbolizing wealth and long life.

Narcissus Festival, sponsored by the Chinese Chamber of Commerce to preserve Chinese traditions and promote Chinese business, held several weeks before the Chinese New Year.

JAPANESE

History. The first group of 148 Japanese arrived in Honolulu in 1868, but large numbers began arriving in 1885 to offset the growing Chinese population, which threatened to dominate the plantation labor market. King Kalakaua himself took part in directing the welcoming ceremonies, after which the newcomers were transported to their assigned plantations. Over the next few decades, over 200,000 Japanese came to Hawaii. The flow of immigrants tapered off and eventually ceased once Hawaii was annexed to the United States and became subject to its immigration policies.

Ironically, the Japanese, recruited to counter the growing Chinese influence, became a dominant force in island life. Until the mid-1980s, the Japanese were the single largest population in Hawaii and are now surpassed only by Caucasians. They have had a pervasive influence on the customs and lifestyle of Hawaii and remain a major force in political, economic, and professional life.

From the first, the Japanese were the most cohesive and exclusive immigrant population, maintaining their language, religion, holiday observances, and other ways of life. The custom of **picture brides**, the practice of arranging marriages with women still in Japan through intermediaries, came about because of the strong preference of the Japanese to marry within their race. The practice of segregating ethnic labor forces on the plantation helped to reinforce their sense of distinctness.

World War II was a crucial catalyst in speeding up changes that were less obviously taking place before the war. While many Japanese continued to identify with their homeland, they also had become a part of their new home, as it had of them. At the outbreak of the war, nearly two out of every five residents of the Islands were of Japanese descent, and three-fourths of these were *nisei* or second generation, and so Americans by birth. The war forced them to declare their loyalty in a way they had not needed to do previously. Once the initial rush of suspicion following Pearl Harbor subsided, the Japanese left no question as to their political affiliation. One of the most highly decorated military units of the war, the 442nd Regimental Combat Team, made up of Americans of Japanese Ancestry (AJA), distinguished itself in combat in the European theater. Today's 100th Infantry Battalion, a U.S. Army Reserve unit in Hawaii, descends from the 442nd and still carries its motto, "Go for Broke." Following the war, the GI Bill opened the door for many Japanese-American men to attend college and enter the ranks of economic, political, educational, and artistic leadership. In the decades following the war, some Japanese citizens reacted against conforming to American styles of living.

To understand Japanese traditions, it is helpful to know a set of terms by which the generations distinguish themselves. *Issei* are first-generation Japanese, born in Japan and uprooted to Hawaii. Few *issei* are still living. The second generation, the *nisei*, went through the war and was largely responsible for the successful mixing of Japanese and American outlooks. *Sansei* are those of the third generation, and *yonsei,* those of the fourth. Because they have been raised by older generations and yet are themselves thrust into society as a large minority, *sansei* and *yonsei* have had to reach their own style of accommodation between Japanese identity and Hawaii's multi-ethnic American society. This fact has created some stress between older and younger generations.

Values and Traditions. Japanese values grow largely out of group identity and loyalty. The nuclear family identifies itself as a family of a particular kind—Japanese. Avoidance of shame, fulfillment of obligations, meeting the expectations of the older generation and extended community, and hard work are important practices among local Japanese. Other values and traits include an emphasis on organization in both social and business affairs, self-restraint, obedience to parents, education, and getting ahead. One of the reasons for the success of the Japanese in Hawaii may be the similarity between these latter values and those of American society as a whole.

Older generations still observe strict reciprocity in gift giving (see ***giri***) and want young people to marry their own kind. Younger generations, like those of all ethnic groups in the Islands, are less strict about such matters but retain traditions according to family and individual inclinations.

The Japanese way of life appears in the custom of removing of **shoes** before entering a house; in foods such as sushi, sashimi, teriyaki, bento lunches, and ***mochi***; the tea ceremony; use of the *furo* (hot soaking bath) and *futons* (folding cushions to sleep on), and the observance of holidays. The Japanese-American community celebrates:

Cherry Blossom Festival in February
Girls' Day, March 3rd
Buddha Day in April
Boys' Day, May 5th
Bon Festival in July and August
Bodhi Day in December

PORTUGUESE

History. The Portuguese began immigrating in 1878 from the Portuguese-controlled Madeira Islands in the Atlantic, where they were recruited by Hawaii's plantation owners to supplement the growing numbers of Chinese plantation workers. The Portuguese were seen as ideal laborers: sober, hard-working, peaceful, and already adapted to a climate similar to that of Hawaii. About 17,000 persons immigrated to Hawaii from the Madeira Islands. The Portuguese often came as entire families, unlike the Chinese and Japanese.

Even though they were recruited under more favorable terms than other groups, the Portuguese faced many of the same brutal conditions of plantation life, including low pay, hard work, and harsh supervision, all of which fostered a close-knit group identity. However, their racial affiliation with Caucasians set them apart from the Chinese and Japanese laborers and won them an uneasy status somewhere between the bosses and the common laborers. Many Portuguese men became *luna* or overseers, although very few advanced to head overseer. This somewhere-between status has followed the Portuguese off the plantation and into life in modern Hawaii. The Portuguese have felt, with some justification, that those at the top of the social ladder have resisted including them in their ranks. Until 1940, government census documents even distinguished between "Portuguese" and "other Caucasian." Today the Portuguese comprise six percent of the population, and even though they are well represented in skilled trades, they may still be underrepresented in the professional fields.

Values and Traditions. Portuguese customs and family traditions can be traced to their Roman Catholic, Southern European roots. The Portuguese value strong families, with authority centered in the father, though the mother may in fact run the household and control the family budget. Morals, courtship, and marriage adhere to Roman Catholic values.

In the 1950s Portuguese clubs began a revival of their culture, reaching its peak in 1978 during the centennial celebration of their arrival. This revival continues today, marking the resurgence of pride in Portuguese identity and contributions to life in Hawaii.

Because the Portuguese population has always been relatively small, Portuguese visibility in the cultural stream of Hawaii is not readily apparent. Nevertheless, there is a strong imprint. The ***ukulele*** is an island adaptation of a small, guitar-like instrument brought in by the Portuguese. Many pidgin words are adaptations of Portuguese. The intonation patterns of pidgin may also have been influenced by the Madeiran lilt. The tradition of **talking story** is also generally attributed to the Portuguese. The practice of folk medicine by a *curadeira* or healer, usually an elderly woman taught by another practitioner, is still followed in some families. Several island food favorites originated with the Portuguese, including sweet bread, which is frequently sold for fund-raising, and *malasadas*, a delicious treat of sweet dough deep-fat fried and coated with sugar.

OKINAWANS

History. Okinawans, who began immigrating in 1900 and now number close to 40,000, constitute one of Hawaii's most cohesive ethnic subgroups. Many of the original immigrants from Okinawa were married men who pooled their money in *tanomoshi*, or credit groups, to bring their wives and families to Hawaii.

Whereas regional distinctions within the Chinese and Filipino populations have tended to blur with time, Okinawans and *naichi* (Japanese from the main islands of Japan) have to a large extent kept separate identities, mostly because for centuries the *naichi* have looked down their noses at Okinawans. Although immigrants from Okinawa and mainland Japan came to Hawaii for the same reasons and under the same circumstances, the Japanese tended to keep alive old prejudices. Okinawans were viewed as country hicks with rougher physical features. So they were avoided as marriage partners, excluded from business ventures, and sometimes even shut out from Japanese schools and educational recognition.

Outsiders are often surprised that people of apparently the same nationality and culture will preserve regional distinctions so fiercely, but the fact is that Okinawans and Japanese are not really of the same culture. Okinawa lies 400 miles southeast of the nearest island of Japan and was ruled for hundreds of years by China. Okinawans did not speak Japanese, but their own language—a relative of Japanese but not, as some mistakenly thought, just a crude dialect of it. Okinawan dress, diet, and social rituals also differed noticeably from those of Japan.

Prejudices have mellowed in second- and third-generation families, but along the way, the resulting discrimination has unified the

Okinawans to assist each other socially and economically, to carry on their own traditions of dance and worship, and even to wield political power. Recently, politicians of Okinawan descent have organized winning political campaigns on a footing of support from among fellow residents.

Okinawans are often described by comparison to Japanese. Like the Japanese, they are known as a hard-working people with a strong sense of group identity and responsibility. By contrast, they are known as more peaceful, friendly, and gentle.

Many Okinawans belong to clubs called *son-jin-kai* or district associations, organized around the districts and villages from which Hawaii's Okinawans descend. Okinawans sponsor a Hawaii Okinawa Jubilee each July.

FILIPINOS

History. The Filipinos were the last large group of immigrants to arrive under the plantation system of recruitment and employment. They came in three waves: approximately 115,000 between 1906 and 1932; 7,000 in 1946, and the last group after 1965, when a new quota system of immigration began. The enormous numbers in the first few decades meant that by 1920 almost one-third of all plantation workers were Filipino. They faced a situation different from that of earlier immigrant groups in that they had to adapt to an existence already established by preceding immigrants. As one writer has described this,

> The Filipino immigrants had to adapt themselves to the unstable cultural synthesis of the diverse ethnic groups the plantations had assembled for their labor pool. For example, the Filipinos found that they had to learn "pidgin" English in order to deal with plantation labor procedures. Standard English was not particularly useful in that situation, but on the other hand, proficiency in pidgin was hardly advantageous . . . outside the plantation setting.(3)

The waves came from different regions of the Philippines and from different socio-economic backgrounds. Early immigrants came predominantly from the northern Ilocos region and tended to be less literate, while later ones came from diverse regions, including Cebu, and tended to be more educated. While it is an oversimplification to treat the Filipinos as one homogeneous population, the plantation experience had such a similar impact on the majority that it makes sense to treat them as a single group. Their history on the plantation is, like that of other immigrant groups, one of ethnic segregation, hard work governed by a rigid schedule and under bosses usually of other races, economic struggle, labor organization and unrest to achieve equitable pay, social organization overseen by plantation managers, and so on. Still, the vast majority of Filipinos found life in Hawaii preferable to that back home and put off their initial dream of returning.

Values and traditions. Because many Filipino immigrants could not bring with them the extended family structure and its interwoven practices of Filipino Catholicism, they duplicated these as nearly as they could. They formed *partidos* or social alliances, observed *novenas* or nine-day periods of devotion at special times, and sponsored baptisms and weddings. Alliances filled the void of extended families with networks of friends who could be counted on to help with loans or labor, give advice, and take part in important events when social interaction was desired. A clearly understood philosophy of reciprocal obligation cemented those in a particular alliance. To turn down a request for assistance meant placing oneself above the network of friends; equally, to give assistance meant that one could expect to receive help in return when one needed it. One way of making visible the expectations of the *partido* or alliance was to ask others to stand as sponsors (god-parents) at a child's baptism or to solicit extensive help for a wedding banquet.

Filipino values, like those of other groups in Hawaii, are changing and evolving. The older generations place strong emphasis on the fulfillment of obligations, the security of the family, improving the financial and social status of the family as a legacy to the next generation, and avoiding shameful and antisocial behavior. Selfishness is especially frowned on. Someone who ignores or exploits the group to look good or get ahead invites community disapproval.

As families have left the plantation and raised their Hawaii-born children, some of the traditional expectations and values have naturally weakened. The generation born in Hawaii exhibits motives and values much closer to those of mainstream America while still keeping alive its pride in Filipino identity. Politically, the Filipinos have not wielded power proportionate to their numbers. Nor have they been well represented in the professions.

The Filipino community sponsors:

an annual Miss Hawaii-Filipina Festival

an annual Fiesta Filipina in May

Rizal Day, on December 30 of each year, which celebrates the life of Dr. Jose Rizal, a Filipino writer, physician, and martyr-patriot.

SOUTH PACIFIC ISLANDERS

Samoans. Small numbers of Samoans immigrated to Hawaii early in this century, drawn by economic opportunity, while others came to join the Mormon gathering at Laie, Oahu. Most immigration has occurred since World War II. Because American Samoa has been a U.S. Territory since 1900, its people have been free to travel to the U.S. Many American Samoans moved because of their employment as civilian or military personnel of the U.S. Navy, which operated a naval base and a coaling station in American Samoa until 1951. Most families in American Samoa have family ties in the more populous Western Samoa, making it possible for citizens of the latter to immigrate with their help. With the lure of better jobs and a freer lifestyle, many Samoans have left the South Pacific, settling primarily in Hawaii and California. At present, more persons of Samoan ancestry live outside Samoa than within.

The Samoan people are proud to be Samoan. Samoan culture is somewhat comparable to the Hawaiian, but more authoritarian. Samoans value their *aiga* or extended family, and their village, both of which are organized under *matai* or chiefs. A village council rules by consensus over a wide range of matters. Group welfare is generally valued over individual fulfillment. In nearly all matters of family and personal relations, traditional Samoans emulate the *Faa Samoa* or Samoan way.

Certain inherent tensions within the Samoan way are more

successfully managed in the native village than outside Samoa. In the village, the authority structure and community social pressure keep a rein on the aggressive tendencies that some anthropologists say are an integral part of Samoan culture. Outside Samoa, the clash with Western culture and the lack of socially imposed restrictions may aggravate these aggressive tendencies. Samoans stress submission to authority, cooperation, and a kind of social wisdom that leads to proper behavior or performance in a given situation. But the dynamics of village political life also favor, within limits, those who achieve status by asserting their abilities. Physical discipline is common and may go beyond the bounds considered tolerable by most other cultures. Samoan families in Hawaii often experience considerable stress as they try to pass on Samoan values without the kind of support and control the home village makes possible.

Samoans in Hawaii celebrate Samoa Day in April and Samoa Flag Raising Day in July. The ***lavalava***, a versatile cloth wrap-around, is actually a South Pacific article and not of Hawaii origins.

Tongans. Even though Tonga does not have similar territorial ties with the United States, as does Samoa, its citizens have proved equally mobile. Beginning in the 1970s, sizeable communities sprang up in Hawaii and California as Tongans left home to escape unemployment, limited educational opportunities, and the near impossibility of owning land. About 8,000 now reside in Hawaii. A major source of revenue to the Kingom of Tonga is money sent home by expatriate family members.

Tongans are known as a generous, friendly, and hard-working people, with a great capacity for warm enthusiasm and spontaneous enjoyment. Facing language barriers and cultural differences, the Tongans have held fast to their highly developed traditions of song, poetry, mutual assistance, and avid competition. Though they live away from their home islands, Tongans in Hawaii are proud that their nation is one of the last on the globe to be ruled by a king and a parliament.

OTHER GROUPS

Hawaii's diverse population includes a sprinkling of other peoples who, though fewer in number, have also left their distinctive mark on modern Hawaii's culture.

Blacks. Blacks have a long history in Hawaii. Anthony Allen, a former black slave from New York, landed in Hawaii in 1810, married a Hawaiian woman, and gained considerable wealth and prominence. Betsy Stockton arrived as a free black with the missionaries in 1823 and helped found the Lahainaluna school on Maui. Several hundred blacks from Louisiana and Alabama were recruited as plantation workers in 1901. Larger numbers came with the military. A black army regiment was stationed in Hawaii in 1913. Greater numbers came during and after World War II and, of these, some stayed on or returned because of the racial tolerance and the natural beauty. About 19,000 blacks now live in the Islands and provide leaders in business, politics, labor, defense, and sports.

Koreans. Koreans number about 18,000, or about two percent of the state's population. Most local Koreans descend from immigrants who arrived from 1903 to 1905, when the Hawaii Sugar Planters Association was—as ever—looking for new sources of cheap labor. Many of these immigrants were Christian, having been converted in their homeland and recruited through their congregations. With less restrictive contracts, they were soon able to seek the most advantageous employment, often away from the plantation. Though they came planning to stay only temporarily, most of the original group stayed on after Japan's 1910 annexation of Korea made their return home less desirable than settling in Hawaii. Their strong cohesion in protesting Japanese rule of their homeland helped solidify them, yet this cohesion has not carried over into their marriage patterns: Koreans have one of the highest rates of inter-ethnic marriage in the Islands. Their passion for education has led to notable success. They have one of the highest average incomes of all of Hawaii's sub-populations and are well represented in the professional fields.

Spanish. Large numbers of Spanish-speaking people have come to Hawaii. Eight thousand arrived with the Portuguese immigrants in the first decade of the 1900s. Most of them left for California as soon as they could; a few remained in Hawaii, where they have generally been seen by others as blending in with the Portuguese and the Puerto Ricans. The latter group came to Hawaii at about the same time as the Koreans; those who stayed assimilated Hawaiian culture rapidly until today only a few thousand identify themselves as Puerto Ricans.

Southeast Asians. An additional immigrant group of growing importance has arrived from Southeast Asia. Mostly Vietnamese, this group also includes Laotians, Cambodians, and Hmongs. Unlike others who have immigrated to Hawaii in modern times, many have come as refugees, and this fact no doubt makes their adjustment to life in the Islands as psychologically difficult as that of earlier agricultural workers. By external measures they are doing very well, taking full advantage of education and free enterprise to lay a groundwork for the prosperity and independence of future generations. Their contribution to Hawaii's culture so far is small, except for the growing popularity of Thai and Vietnamese cuisine. In a larger sense, though, they are reenacting a central story of Hawaiian history, of a people uprooted and set down in a new social, political, and economic setting, fashioning a new life and achieving success through sacrifice, hard work, and intelligent exploitation of opportunity.

ALPHABETICAL GUIDE TO LOCAL CUSTOMS

'AINA • The land.

To Hawaiians *'aina* means much more than real estate. It means the land as a nurturer, a partner in the cycles of life, and a dwelling place that must be revered. The land supports and sustains; in return, it must be given respect and caring.

Environmentalists instinctively understand the meaning of *'aina,* but there is much more to the Hawaiian perspective than appreciating and preserving the beauty of the earth. *'Aina* is earth mother, that which feeds. Dr. Emmett Aluli, a Hawaiian activist, defines *'aina* as "a god-given gift that must be treated with respect and dignity" and *aloha 'aina* as "a spiritual, life-sustaining relationship with the land." He explains that the land once served as a source of identity and power among the Hawaiians. The loss of their land separated them from its forces and "dealt them a deathly blow—

physically, psychologically, spiritually." The Hawaiian hunger for land today is not simply an economic one, but a desire for strength, dignity, and identity.

As a newcomer, learn to show respect for the land. An easy demonstration is to pick up litter—yours and others'—at the beach or park. Don't be shocked, though, when some local people seem to disregard this rule. Set an example (and don't lecture, unless you're willing to risk "stink-eye"). Dr. Aluli attributes carelessness for the land to lack of pride and self-esteem.(4)

ALOHA

A word with many meanings, *aloha* is one of the most used and abused words in Hawaii. Life-long friends speak the word fondly at parting, casual acquaintances say it congenially at social gatherings, public speakers pronounce it roundly to begin a speech, audiences repeat it back to public speakers, and tour guides may bark it with barely concealed disdain to groups of low-budget tourists at the airport.

Some critics of modern Hawaii even consider the *aloha* spirit to be nothing more than a marketing ploy to entice tourists to part with their money more readily. But however it is commercially abused, *aloha* is not a marketing invention. It means love, good wishes, compassion, welcome, goodbye, and caring affection—all as real as any marketplace. *Aloha* is now used mostly as a greeting, but its connotations are better conveyed in the expression, "I have a lot of *aloha* for Auntie Pearl" or "She is full of *aloha*." In this sense, it means a spirit of love, acceptance, sharing, and genuine caring. If you can grasp the spirit of *aloha*, you will be on your way to understanding many facets of local, and especially Hawaiian, ways. And the key is this: it is not simply a word to be defined. A feeling of the heart must go along with the understanding of the head. Goodwill and acceptance help create this feeling; beyond that, *aloha* requires a sense of belonging to others and of sharing a common humanity, even if family or racial lines differ.

Incidentally, a 1986 act of the State Senate called on state leaders to exercise the *aloha* spirit in carrying out their functions and wielding power for and over the people. Was this an empty political gesture, or a sincere reminder that civic leaders must care for their constituents as human beings?

ALOHA FRIDAY

Many firms allow their employees to "dress down" and wear *aloha* attire the last day—"Aloha Friday"—of each week, but this hasn't always been the case. The custom has an interesting history tied to the growth of Hawaii's clothing industry.

Until the 1940s, most clothing of local design was sold to visitors. Big firms in the Islands preferred their male employees to wear suits and ties. When Aloha Week was established in 1947, its backers recognized that Hawaii's business could benefit if Hawaii-made clothing became popular among residents. Proponents of Aloha Week saw it as "crucial in selling Hawaiian garments not only to the tourist market, but also to residents, who were encouraged to don the colorful products of local industry during the week's festivities."(5) The City and County of Honolulu allowed men to wear sports shirts—but not of a loud, colorful kind—on the job in the late forties. By the sixties, the fashion barrier weakened further. The Bank of Hawaii became the first major corporation to allow *aloha* attire on Fridays; many other large firms, including the **Big Five**, gradually went along. Now it is rare to find a business or government agency that does not follow the practice of Aloha Friday.

ALOHA 'OE

One of the most beautiful and best-known songs in the Islands, *"Aloha 'Oe"* was composed by Queen Lili'uokalani during an outing to Nu'uanu. Seeing a young couple embracing and saying goodbye, and thinking of her own group's imminent parting, she composed this song. Today it is sung when people say farewell.

Aloha 'Oe

Ha'aheo e ka ua i na pali
(The rain proudly sweeps by the cliffs)
Ke nihi ae la i kanahele
(And passes softly through the trees)
E uhai ana paha i ka liko
(It seems to seek out the buds)
Pua ahihi lehua o uka
(Of the *ahihi lehua* flower in the valley)
Aloha 'oe, aloha 'oe
(Farewell to thee, farewell to thee)
E ke onaona noho i ka lipo

(Thou sweet one who dwells in the forest)
One fond embrace, *a ho'i ae au*
(Now before I go)
Until we meet again

AUMAKUA · Family gods.

Historically, every Hawaiian clan felt a special relationship with certain animals or objects they considered to be their family gods. While these gods did not rank with the higher gods such as Kane and Lono, they brought spiritual powers to a personal level and tied people to the forces of nature. The *aumakua* were felt to be the spirits of ancestors, so that members of a family might consider themselves literally encompassed by ***'ohana***, living and dead. *Aumakua* worked in partnership with the living. Family gods could "protect, warn, counsel, heal, forgive, avenge, and discipline." In return, family members revered, heeded, and made offerings to these lesser gods.(6) As cultural experts have expressed this idea:

> The Hawaiians lived within the close relationships of the *'ohana* (family or clan); the *aumakua* remained members of the clan. The *'ohana* invested family authority in its senior members; the *aumakua* as spiritual ancestors were certainly seniors. With one's *aumakua*, a human-to-spirit communication was possible. One spoke to an *aumakua* through ritual and reverence, but without the almost paralyzing awe the *akuas* or impersonal gods sometimes inspired.(7)

Common *aumakua* were the eel, sea cucumber, turtle, shark, lizard, and species of birds, fish, and insects. Specific trees, plants, rocks, and carved images were also family gods. When a person married, he or she would want to know the *aumakua* of the spouse and would consider the family gods allied just as the two families were. Through this process, families could accumulate dozens of *aumakua*.

BABY LU'AU · See **FIRST BIRTHDAY**.

BIG FIVE

Five large corporations achieved such power in Hawaii that

they nearly entered the realm of myth. All of them had their base in the sugar industry but later extended their activities into other branches of business, including public utilities, pineapples, banking, insurance, shipping, and hotels. Since World War II, as more large mainland firms have established offices and outlets in Hawaii, the near-monopolistic power of the Big Five has diminished. The Big Five were American Factors (Amfac), C. Brewer and Company, Alexander and Baldwin, Castle and Cooke, and Theo. H. Davies.

BODHI DAY

Bodhi Day, celebrated in December, commemorates the enlightenment of Siddhartha Gautama, who founded Buddhism. After a youth of wealth and pleasure, Gautama suddenly recognized the suffering around him and left his family to seek a deeper meaning in existence. While meditating under a bodhi tree, he received enlightened understanding, which became the basis for the teachings of Buddhism.

Bodhi Day is celebrated through services at Buddhist temples. These often include a joint service held by followers of several branches of Buddhism at one temple.

BON FESTIVAL

This festival occurs in July and August to honor the souls of the departed. Family members visit graves, participate in *Bon* dances, and light floating lanterns. The name *Bon* is one of several variations with the same meaning: *Bon-odori, Urabon*, and *Obon*.

The festival has roots in legends of a worthy Buddhist disciple who asked to glimpse the state of his dead mother and saw with horror that she was tormented for a misdeed during her life. The son was moved with pity and asked that her suffering be relieved. His own merit was allowed to compensate for her error. Released from her punishments, she danced joyfully and offered food. The dancing and music of the *Bon* Festival similarly bring the community together in memory of departed loved ones.

In Hawaii, *Bon* dances are coordinated by the Hawaii Buddhist Council, with member temples sponsoring them each weekend during the festival period. *Bon* dances are open to all, but those participating should take time to attend a few practice sessions and dress in *happi* coats or in *kimono*, the traditional full-length Japanese robe-like garment. Dances vary from one temple or *Bon*-dance club to another, but are usually performed in lines or formations around a *yagura* or music tower decorated in bright colors and banners, and to the accompaniment of *taiko* drums, gongs, singing, and instrumental music, live or recorded.

A good place to observe the Floating Lanterns Festival is at the Jodo Mission in Haleiwa. Following a *Bon* dance toward the end of the festival period in August, services are held at the Mission to honor the deceased. After the service, participants carry floating lanterns to the water's edge, light the candles, and release them along with a larger boat lantern which leads the way to paradise. In sending off the floating lanterns, people signify that they wish those who have died to have a peaceful and safe journey to their next existence.(8)

BOYS' DAY

Boys' Day is a Japanese festival celebrated May 5 in honor of boys.

The central feature of Boys' Day celebration is the flying of colorful *koi nobori* or carp streamers. In addition, some families set out displays of male dolls and armor and serve special foods. These items have special symbolism.

Even more important than the use of peach blossoms to represent femininity at Girls' Day is the central role of the carp

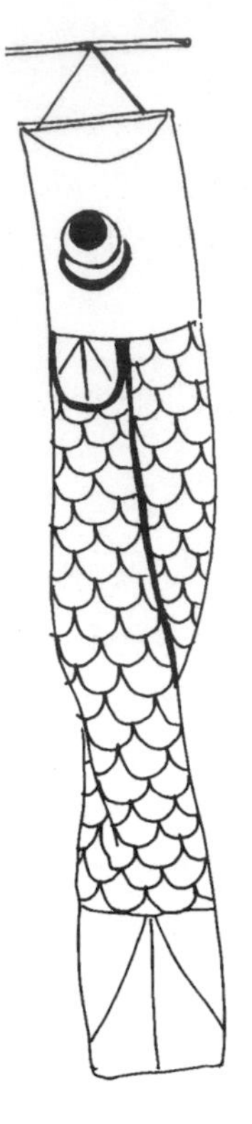

in representing masculinity at Boys' Day. . . .

The tradition of the carp as a symbol of masculinity originated in China. The carp is believed to be able to swim upstream against a strong current and even to be able to surmount waterfalls. Chinese tradition has it that a yellow carp that manages to best the waterfalls of the Yellow River turns into a dragon . . . Apart from its putative prowess as a swimmer, the carp is also believed to have a long life, some living over a hundred years. Small wonder that its qualities of strength, perseverance, and longevity have earned it a central role in Boys' Day.

Koi nobori or carp streamers are of paper or cloth and are fashioned in the form of the carp; they may reach up to twenty feet in length. The streamers are gaily colored, as are the carp themselves, for this fish has been carefully bred so as to possess a great variety of colors and combinations of colors. . . . Carp streamers can be bought in local stores specializing in Japanese goods.

Many families with young sons hang small paper carp inside the house and long fabric carp on tall poles in the front garden. Businesses owned or run by Japanese-Americans hang *koi nobori* outside their stores or offices. It is a delight to see these colorful streamers fluttering in the trade winds of Hawaii.

In addition to flying carp streamers at Boys' Day, some families with male children set up displays of weapons and armor, and also of dolls, as in the case of Girls' Day, except that in this case the dolls are all male—warriors, knights, courtiers, martial arts figures, and so on. *Samurai* dolls were particularly favored in Japan as part of the tradition of instilling a martial spirit in the male segment of the population. They are less favored in Hawaii.

As part of the Boys' Day celebration, some families

continue the custom of serving a few special dishes. These include the same specialties served to celebrate Girls' Day, with the addition of *chimaki*, a cake of rice, soybeans, flour, sugar, and salt, and *kashiwa mochi*, a specially shaped delicacy said to have taken its shape from a *samurai* helmet.(9)

BRIDAL TEA CEREMONY · See CHINESE WEDDING.

BUDDHA DAY

This day celebrates the birthday of Siddhartha Gautama, the enlightened religious leader who became Buddha. It is celebrated on April 8 in Hawaii with special services at some Buddhist temples and by a large public program sponsored by the Hawaii Buddhist Council.

For practitioners who attend these services, an important ceremony centers on a small statue of Buddha set up in a flower temple. Persons attending pour sweet tea over the Buddha figure to commemorate the rain that fell at his birth.

CALABASH COUSINS

Calabash cousins are people considered as family (see ***'ohana***), even though they may have no blood relation. Usually these people have been raised in the same household or in close proximity. In other words, they have eaten from the same calabash and have shared the host family's lot, be it plenty or poverty. A calabash is a gourd or wooden bowl used in this case to prepare or serve food.

CHANTS

Part prayer, part celebration, part projection of spiritual power, chants once formed an integral part of everyday life in Hawaiian culture. Religion was not a separate activity to the Hawaiians—there was not even a word for it—but was threaded inseparably into every facet of life. Chants were a means of addressing the gods and of achieving power in all areas of life. Chants used word power to influence life. They carried *mana* or spiritual force if uttered properly. Chants also preserved knowledge in a culture without writing. Many were sacred and were passed from one generation to another word-for-word. Some chants were the exclusive right of individual classes of *ali'i* or nobility and *kahuna* or priests and were *kapu* or forbidden to anyone else. Some were meant to accompany activities like planting, fishing, or performing group labor.

Chants were used to change conditions of someone's life, pronounce or lift a curse, free someone from a *kapu*, maintain family history, praise someone, mourn, declare love, preserve genealogy, and accomplish many other purposes. Such great power was attributed to the word that if some chants were uttered incorrectly, they could have disastrous consequences for the community. Some assert that in times past a person could be punished by death for mistakes in chanting.

The Hawaiian word for chant is *oli.* This kind differs from *mele,* the more rhythmical and musical songs and recitations that may be sung or used to accompany a *hula. Oli* are usually performed as unaccompanied solos with only two or three tones; *mele* are accompanied and may use four or five tones. Five styles of chanting have been passed down that vary in pitch, voice quality, and rhythm according to the occasion.

An elderly Hawaiian woman remembers the training for young people selected to learn chants: They were taken down to the tidal pools by an elderly chanter and asked to lie down facing the water with their lips an inch from the surface. In this position, they practiced chanting, articulating sounds without making the water ripple from the expelled air. In this way they learned to be heard distinctly while sustaining their breath through long phrases.

Today, chants are heard on only a few of the myriad occasions that used to require them. The most common is the accompaniment of *hula.* Another is a blessing for a construction site or new building by a Hawaiian *kahuna* or priest. Chants may also occasionally be heard at funerals and commemorations.

CHERRY BLOSSOM FESTIVAL

Each year the Honolulu Japanese Junior Chamber of Commerce (HJJCC) sponsors the Cherry Blossom Festival to promote the cultural heritage of Japan, stimulate leadership in the youth of Japanese ancestry, and foster commerce. The festival events are spread out over several months but usually reach their peak near the early part of April. The events change from year to year but always include a beauty and talent pageant for young women, entertainment from both East and West, and an international trade show. Other events may include cooking classes, flower-arranging demonstrations, tea ceremony exhibitions, songfest, *origami* or paper folding, films, gardening demonstrations, music, *mochi* pounding, and martial arts.

The Cherry Blossom Queen and her court, selected through interviews and performances, are crowned at the Coronation Ball. The Queen then tours Japan, sponsored by the HJJCC, on behalf of the Japanese-Americans of Hawaii.

CHINESE DINNER • See NINE-COURSE DINNER.

CHINESE MEDICINE

A Chinese drugstore offers the results of thousands of years of study and practice in the use of herbs and animal substances to cure ailments and regulate health. Historically, the Chinese attributed properties to all kinds of foods and plants, making little distinction between food and what we would now call medicine or drugs. Modern Chinese druggists are the heirs to this information and so can prescribe herbs and other substances for anything from a fever to a weak heart. One local Chinese physician listed the following remedies and their use: seaweed for goiter, lotus nodes for bleeding, mushrooms for memory, raw ginko nut for tumors, and loquat leaves for blood pressure. Additionally, an herbalist might prescribe ginger for a cough, sesame seed for sex appeal, garlic for heart problems, corn silk for bladder and kidneys, and wood ear fungus for blood clotting. More exotic remedies include tiger bone for aches and pains, velvet of deer horn for deafness, cicada for fever, and deer horn for increased sexual potency.(10)

CHINESE NEW YEAR

Also known as Lunar New Year, this holiday celebrates the New Year as calculated under the lunar calendar. It comes in late January or early February. Like Western New Year festivities, those of the Chinese New Year mark an end and a beginning and so are full of hopes for prosperity, luck, and successful relations with family and friends.

The most noticeable (because it is the noisiest) part of the celebration is the use of **fireworks**. Until recently, firecrackers and other kinds of explosive fireworks were readily available at New Year; however, safety concerns led Honolulu City and County to limit their use. Now one needs a special permit, available through the fire department, to purchase and ignite fireworks.

Chinese New Year is observed with ***mochi*** cake, called *nien-gao,* a family dinner, fireworks, and the exchange of money wrapped in red paper. The money, called ***li-see***, brings good luck.

The customary greeting for the occasion is *"kung hee fat choy!"*

CHINESE WEDDING

Traditionally, marriage among the Chinese has been less the celebration of individual, romantic choice than in Western societies. Rather, it marks the binding of families and the promise of continuing ancestral lines. Elaborate Chinese wedding customs have evolved to integrate the bride into the family of the groom and to bind both families in such a way as to make future separation difficult. The color red dominates in costumes and decorations, as if to signify that fertility and creation of a posterity are of uppermost concern, whereas white, signifying purity, dominates in Western marriage ceremonies.

Not many Chinese in Hawaii preserve the full wedding tradition, but many do observe the bridal tea ceremony which has long been a part of it. It should be noted that tea occupies a special place in most oriental cultures. Following the wedding ceremony, the two families gather in a room where a decorated table is filled with pomelos and oranges, dried fruit, and sticky cake or *gao*. The bride dresses in traditional embroidered silks and proceeds as follows:

> She goes around to pour tea for her in-laws and relatives. For the bridal cup of tea with candied fruit, the bride receives a generous *li-see* or money with good wishes and good luck from each person served. After the first round, the bride pours everyone tea for the second time for added good luck. The tea

pouring follows the traditional order, i.e., serving the in-laws first and then the bride's own family next. For each generation, the male is always served before the female.(11)

CHING MING

During this Chinese festival, known as the Festival of Pure Brightness and celebrated on April 5, some Chinese families set up food offerings at the graves of their loved ones. Tradition calls for a roasted pig to be placed at the grave; afterwards all the food is taken home and eaten. If you wish to respectfully watch this practice, visit the Manoa Chinese Cemetery on the weekend after April 5.

What is the meaning of the festival? During Ching Ming, the gates of heaven open for thirty days, allowing dead ancestors to pass through. The living greet and honor them with food and visits to grave sites.

COCK FIGHTING

Cock fighting was brought to the Islands by Filipino immigrants. Although it has long been illegal in Hawaii, this gambling sport did serve important functions in plantation villages. To men who worked six days a week, it provided excitement, risk, and aggressive activity. Watching two fighting cocks fly at each other with razor-sharp gaffs or knives on their legs provided thrills for men who spent most of the week carrying out bosses' orders. And a man could gain prestige breeding and raising game cocks or betting shrewdly.

Cock fighting still takes place in rural and plantation communities, where "houses" (small groups of men who organize and manage the facility and the betting) control the sport for a small percentage of the money changing hands. Bettors wager from $5 or $10 up to $2,000, influenced by factors such as a bird's bloodlines, its record of wins, its breeder, feeder, handler, and even the person who ties the gaff on the chicken's left leg. For unevenly matched birds, a system of handicaps dictates how high or low the knife will be placed on the leg.

The fight itself proceeds in the following way. Two specially bred chickens fitted with gaffs are first placed near each other to attract mutual attention, then released from opposite sides of a dirt arena or "pit." From there, they fly to attack each other and are then separated and placed on the attack again, until the referee declares one of the roosters dead. The losing rooster has its left leg severed so that the gaff can be returned to its owner, but the rooster itself becomes the property of the winning bird's owner, who usually takes it home to cook it in the pot.

Because cock fighting is illegal, it comes under various degrees of police surveillance, depending on the county's vigilance against the sport and the rise and fall of public opposition. Police are hampered by the difficulty of proving that persons present at a cock fight are actually the owners, referees, or bettors. Arrest of these participants requires physical evidence or eyewitnesses, which are hard to come by once the alarm spreads to those at the pit. To avoid repeat offenses and thus higher fines, principal organizers and competitors have been known to arrange for others without arrest records to take the heat for them, paying all fines and penalties.

Supporters of cock fighting point out that boxing is no less brutal than their sport, yet boxing pits humans—members of a supposedly intelligent species—against each other at the risk of blood and broken bones.

COOKBOOKS • See the end of the entry on **FOOD.**

CRACK SEED

Walk into any snack or food store in Hawaii and you'll see a rack of the most unusual tart, tangy, sour, sweet, and salty snack foods to be found anywhere on the planet. Locally, these go by the name "crack seed."

The story of crack seed is woven into the story of Chinese family business, and both stories reveal much about the "flavor" of life in Hawaii. Although other companies make and sell crack seed (Jade Food Products, for example, claims to be the only local company that prepares seed rather than imports it), the Yick Lung Company dominates the market and is largely responsible for making crack seed an indispensable stash-in-the-pocket goody for locals. The Yick Lung Co. operates squarely in the tradition of Chinese family business. In fact, the company is now in the hands of the third generation of family owner-managers and will soon bring the fourth generation into the operation—once the way of the future has completed college.

In 1900, the Chinese immigrant Yee Sheong opened a little store on Lusitana Street selling salted plums—*li hing mui* in Chinese—from large glass jars. *Li hing mui* was a centuries-old food from the home country. Its name in Chinese, "traveling plum," came from hundreds of years back, when Chinese warriors were given salted plums as part of their rations because they could be carried and eaten over a long period of time. Yee made a number of different savory sauces for his plums and dispensed them by the scoop into brown paper packages. Old-timers here can still remember eating *li hing mui* and turning the brown paper inside out to lick the last of the flavorful sauce from the paper.

Yee's store was a success, so he bought a horse and buggy, and later a Ford Model T truck, to take his business to the streets. By this time, his son Frederick worked in the business and saw greater potential by packaging and distributing the various flavors of *li hing mui* and other unusual flavored snacks that had been produced. In the 1940s people all over the Islands started tasting crack seed.

The name "crack seed" actually derives from one variety of salted plum that Frederick had produced and marketed. He named all his items descriptively. One variety featured plum with the pit cracked to give it greater flavor in combination with the sweet and sour sauce in which it was marinated. This variety was dubbed "Crack Seed." Somehow, this name caught on and came to be applied to all varieties of the snack, whether or not they contained seed or plum. Today, a surprising array of flavors and types of crack seed can be found in mom-and-pop neighborhood shops, drugstores, supermarkets, small street businesses, or mall outlets selling nothing but crack seed, packaged or scooped from jars in the old way.

The most popular types among local kids are the old standard *li hing mui*, rock salt plum (soaked plum with Hawaiian rock salt), mango seed, and lemon peel. For something more unusual, try sweet and sour lemon peel or red ginger. Some people stick a rock salt plum or *li hing mui* in the middle of an orange or lemon and then squeeze and suck the juice around the seed.

Unlike other snack foods like popcorn or potato chips, crack seed is not meant to be chomped and swallowed quickly. Rather, it should be slowly nibbled and held in the mouth as the flavoring and fruit reveal their taste. Like local life.

DA KINE

A versatile pidgin phrase that simply means, "whatever I'm referring to." It can be a euphemism for a delicate subject or body part, or it can mean something more ordinary. So, "Hey, you bring *da kine*?" can mean anything from "You got the *pakalolo*?" to "Do you have the computer program?"

DAY IN JAPAN

A program scheduled during the summer featuring Japanese

culture. Day in Japan offers an excellent introduction to many customs and arts as practiced in Japan. These include the tea ceremony, traditional music and dance, flower arranging, the dressing of a bride in formal *kimono*, and so on.

DIRECTIONS

You can just about forget north, south, east, and west in giving directions in Hawaii. People here tend to think in terms of *makai* (toward the water) and *mauka* (inland, or toward the mountains). In Honolulu, two other terms are useful: *Ewa* (pronounced "ehvah"), which means toward the direction of Ewa, on the southwest coast of Oahu, and Diamond Head, which means toward that landmark. Waikiki is Diamond Head of downtown, but Ewa of Kahala.

FIREWORKS

Until a few years ago, Hawaii was boys' heaven—fireworks, including firecrackers, were legal and freely available on New Year's Eve, Chinese New Year, and the 4th of July. It was not unusual to see long strings of firecrackers hanging from poles and wires around the neighborhood, set off one after another and leaving the streets covered with shredded paper.

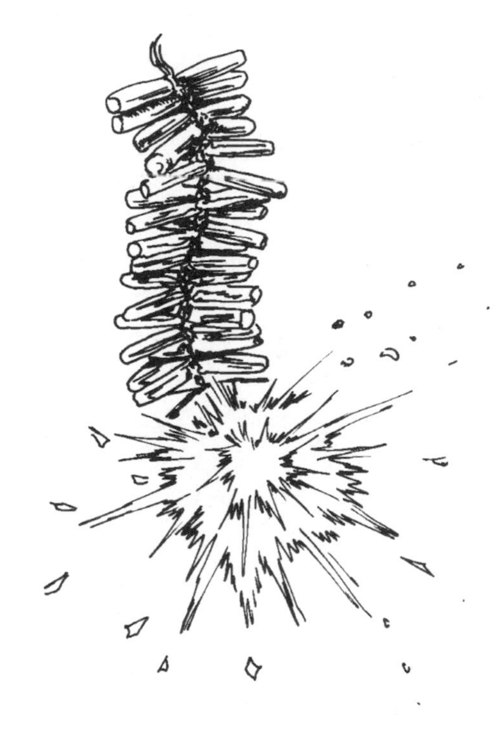

The reason for this unusual legal indulgence was the religious significance of fireworks to the Chinese, for whom the loud sputter of firecrackers drove away evil spirits at special times of the year. In 1983, the Honolulu City Council restricted, for safety and health reasons, the sale and use of fireworks but left a loophole to pay homage to the religious overtones and tradition.

To buy fireworks, obtain a permit from the fire department at least five working days before New Year's Eve, Chinese New Year, and the 4th of July. No fee is required, but the permit imposes restrictions on when, where, and how the fireworks may be set off. On Oahu, the permit may be obtained at any fire station. On neighbor islands, different ordinances apply, so call the appropriate fire department for information.

FIRST BIRTHDAY

Many local families (especially those of Hawaiian ancestry) put on a big party or *lu'au* on a child's first birthday. One might wonder why, since one-year-old children don't know what a birthday is.

For some families, a first birthday is just a good excuse to party. Others say the party marks a child's entry into life, now that it has made it through the first year. The latter view is reinforced by traditions of other Polynesian societies that hold feasts to celebrate early birthdays of children, so the tradition of first-birthday *lu'au* probably goes way back in time. This celebration, called the *'aha'aina palala* in ancient Hawaii, was held in honor of the first-born child. It "expressed the *aloha* of all the relatives and friends. . . . This *aloha* was expressed in the form of gifts to the child, and in the composition of chants (*mele*) which were performed with dances (*hula*). The feast, enjoyed by all who came to honour the *hiapo* [first-born], was an expression of the family's response and pride in the occasion, making it a gay time." (12) Nowadays, family and friends usually make a cash contribution to the host family.

The baby *lu'au* may have become more general after the arrival of Westerners and the introduction of diseases previously unknown to Hawaiians. The infant mortality rate became so high that the perpetuation of the race was threatened. Once a child reached a first birthday, he or she had more than a fifty-fifty chance of surviving.

FOOD

It is true: some people live to eat. And Hawaii gives them a lot to live for. Learning the ways of Hawaii is a culinary adventure for those who enjoy a tremendous variety of ethnic foods. In the Islands these include *sushi, sukiyaki, sashimi,* and *bento* lunches from Japan; *malasadas* and sweet bread from Portugal; *kim chee* and barbecued beef strips from Korea; *lumpia* and chicken *adobo* from the Philippines; crack seed and stir fry from China; *kalua* pig, *poi, taro,* and *ulu* or breadfruit from Hawaii. And many delicious combinations are purely local: *hulihuli* chicken, roasted on spits over huge beds of wood charcoal; plate lunches; spam and rice; chili and rice; and many more.

For all its variety, food in Hawaii fills a role beyond that of feeding and pleasure. It symbolizes generosity and sharing, the plenitude of life, and the commonality of human experience. When you enter a local home, don't be surprised if you're invited to share in eating whatever has been served at the latest meal. Eat something, even just a bit. Take something of your hosts' into yourself. And when you visit someone, build similar bonds by taking something to eat with you. Don't worry about what to take, anything will do: rice, fruit, a bottle of punch syrup, pastries, leftover barbecue, and so on. People will remember and extend *aloha* in your direction. It doesn't matter whether they have plenty already. What matters is that you thought to bring something.

You may hear the remark: "If people offer you something, take it or they might get offended." Remove the condescending tone from this statement, and there is a kernel of truth in it. To turn down a tasty bit can appear as rejection of the people who offer it. One woman told that when a newcomer-guest turns down her food, she wonders whether the person considers it not good enough, or not cleanly prepared. At large gatherings such as *lu`au*, some outsiders make sour faces and roll their eyes to each other in what they think is a private joke over unfamiliar dishes. Their joke is neither private nor funny to hosts and other guests.

In Hawaii, food served by different ethnic groups, particularly at holiday observances, symbolizes aspects of life. Many Chinese dishes have names or legends associated with them that give the foods special meaning. *Fat choi*, a kind of algae, indicates wealth; *jun see* or long rice indicates long life; *foo jook* or bean sticks indicate blessings to the household; *bak ko* or *ginko* nut indicates numerous grandchildren; and *how see* or oysters indicate a good occasion.

Some newcomers are surprised at the spread put on by families of modest means when they host a birthday or graduation *lu'au.* Providing food of great variety and quantity is the family's way of acknowledging the bounty of life and nourishing friendships. They do it knowing that other friends will do the same, even if they, too, stretch their budgets to the limit. Local families also know they can count on close relatives and friends to help provide a feast. Perhaps one cousin will offer to bring fish; another, *taro* or breadfruit; and another, long rice.

A local friend confided that she and her friends sometimes watch newcomers to see how generous they are when asked to bring food to a social gathering. Many residents who have grown up elsewhere have a tendency to bring a token offering: a pitifully small salad or jello, a bag of chips, etc. If you want to show local guests and friends that your heart is a giving one, start by going beyond the minimum when it's your turn to bring food.

If you want to become adept at cooking local dishes, a number of books can help you learn. *Hawaii's Spam Cookbook*, by Ann Corum, has 98 recipes for this island favorite. *Pupus: Adaptations,* by Sachi Fukuda, will guide you in preparing over a hundred local *hors d'oeuvres. Kau Kau Kitchen*, by Dana Black, provides down-home recipes for family cooking and entertaining. *E Ho'olako Mau*, by Tamar Luke, contains a collection of recipes favored by Hawaiians. As its title suggests ("Continue to Enrich" is its translation), this cookbook also offers insights into the lore of Hawaiian food items and techniques—

including manners for eating *poi*. *E Ho'olako Mau* can be ordered by mail by sending $12.95 to Hawaiian Cookbook, Vol. II, P.O. Box 291, Kaneohe, HI 96744.

FUND RAISING

Hawaii abounds in person-to-person fund raising. Hardly a month passes without someone at work selling tickets for Portuguese sausage or young people at the door selling sweetbread, pizza offers, discount coupons, or carnival tickets. With Hawaii's cost of living and wage levels, all this fund raising fills in the gap that in other places is usually dealt with by school and government budgets.

If you stay long, and especially if you have children in Scouting, band, or sports, you, too, will sell tickets to friends and co-workers who sold to you. And don't be surprised to find that the voluntary aspect of helping raise funds gets a little forgotten. You may wind up with twenty tickets assigned to you and be expected to sell them—or buy them yourself. It's all a part of the give and take of life in Hawaii.

GAMBLING

Got gambling in your blood? According to Las Vegas casino operators and local travel agents, many Hawaii residents do. They travel to Las Vegas to the tune of about 100,000 per year. In the travel section of the newspaper you'll find tour packages, sometimes including airfare, meals, and room for less than it costs to fly round-trip to Los Angeles.

Hawaiian residents are favored customers with several downtown Las Vegas hotels, particularly the California and Fremont, which rely on the Hawaii market for a large percentage of their business. The California targeted the Hawaii market in the mid-seventies and has since booked a high percentage of its rooms to Hawaii. Hotel operators say visitors from Hawaii are ideal clients. They like to gamble; they manage their money well, keeping their bets and losses within the range they can handle; they pay off their debts quickly; and they behave well at the gaming tables. They also come back—some making three or four trips a year.

Why such a steady flow of gamblers to the bright lights? Some guess the reason has to do with a taste for gambling among some ethnic groups (a majority of those who book Las Vegas tours are reportedly of Asian descent). But it may also have to do with the high dollar value of Las Vegas tours and the lure of lights, shows, and food round-the-clock.

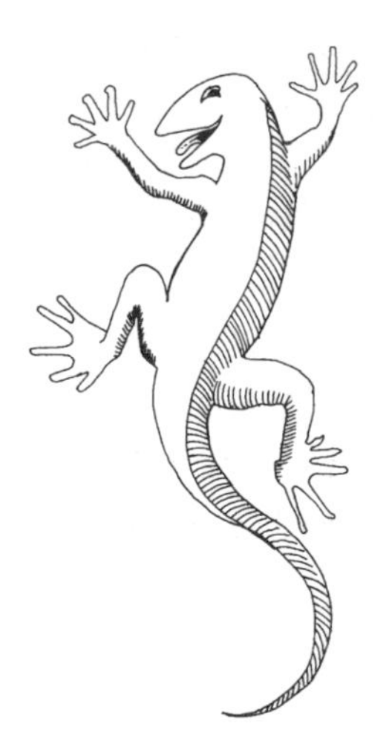

GECKO

A small lizard with large eyes and sticky toes that can do what we only threaten—climb the walls. It is a hospitable creature, willing to share a home or apartment with its owners if, in return, it can feed on insects. It makes a distinctive sound something like a cricket.

Some newcomers react to their first gecko by running from the room screaming about enormous bugs. Whatever your initial reaction, try not to be repulsed by these harmless creatures, even if lizards are the last thing you thought you'd be living with. You can't easily get rid of them. And more important, they eat many times their weight in bugs. Besides, killing a gecko is considered bad luck—to many Hawaiians it is an *aumakua* or family god. Unless you like protecting small cockroaches, leave well enough alone.

GINSENG

Searching for a cure-all? If traditions and legends of the Orient hold true, it has already been found in ginseng, a plant whose large root resembles pale carrots. The shape of the root—it can look something like the trunk and legs of a human—may account for some of the properties attributed to it. Whatever the reason, ginseng has been cultivated for centuries in Asia, and certain varieties are prized for their restorative powers. A well-regulated treatment of ginseng can, it is said, give one more vigor, longer endurance, more resistance to illness, and healing from many specific sicknesses.

GIRI

Japanese for reciprocal obligation.

In feudal Japan *giri* referred to the loyalty binding a *samurai* (knight or warrior) to his lord. In modern Hawaii, the term has a narrower meaning referring to the obligation to reciprocate in the giving of gifts.

When a Japanese person receives a gift—say for a wedding, graduation, funeral, or travel—*giri* is observed when that person makes note of the nature and value of the gift and, on a future occasion, returns to the original givers something of the same value. A completely unsolicited gift may appropriately bring a return of slightly lower value, but gifts for family events are usually reciprocated in value very close to the original.

To those who grew up with more individualistic and spontaneous customs of gift giving, *giri* may seem cold and calculating, but it has virtues of its own. To those who follow it, it becomes not a rigid observance of tit-for-tat, but a recognition of the network of giving and receiving that binds members of a society together.

GIRLS' DAY

This special Japanese day on March 3 of each year is celebrated with ***mochi*** cakes and doll displays. In Japanese the day bears the name *hinamatsuri* or dolls festival.

Girls' Day is observed by many as follows:

As part of the Girls' Day celebration a distinctive diamond-shaped *mochi* known as *hishi-mochi* is sold by local confectionary stores. This *mochi* is said to have originated as an imitation of the diamond shape of a medicinal leaf thought to have the property of giving long life to the eater. While this belief is no longer subscribed to, the shape has been retained in the making of this *mochi*.

The *mochi* given to girls at this time are made in three colors, white, red, and green. White represents the snow of winter, red the flowers of spring, and green the fresh verdure of summer. There is no color for autumn, as it is hoped that there will be no "autumn" in their lives.

Other special foods include *unami*, a dish of cooked vegetables with meat, and *sekihan*, a dish of rice cooked with azuki beans.

As the term *hinamatsuri* indicates, however, the most distinctive feature of Girls' Day is the attention given to dolls.

Families start the collection of display dolls at the birth of a girl-child. At each succeeding Girls' Day, new dolls are added.

The basic collection includes two court figures, most often the emperor and empress, three ladies-in-waiting, five musicians, two retainers, and three guards. On each Girls' Day the dolls, many in glass cases, are brought out and placed on shelves in the order mentioned; bowls and plates of food are set before them.

The custom of adding dolls to the collection and displaying them on each succeeding Girls' Day is practiced especially in families in which grandmothers are still around to carry on the tradition. Quite a few younger people also preserve this custom, however, and many people of all ages have one or two dolls in glass cases on permanent display.(13)

HANAI • Adoption, Hawaiian style.

The term *hanai* can mean to adopt or to place a child with relatives, or it can refer to the foster child. The Hawaiian population formerly practiced *hanai* extensively; now it is less common. As part of the ***'ohana*** system, *hanai* allowed relatives to share in caring for children. Sometimes a child was given to another family to fulfill an obligation, as when grandparents took over raising the first-born child of their own married children. In this case the child was considered rightfully to belong to the grandparents and to have been brought into the world for them. Sometimes *hanai* filled a gap left in a family not able to have children or in a family deprived of a child through death. Sometimes it relieved a family of an unwanted child or lifted heavy burdens of childcare.

Outsiders have difficulty understanding how parents could allow a child to leave home permanently, but it should be remembered that this was not an anonymous process for getting a child out of the way. Even when the motive was to make life easier for parents, the child went to relatives and, therefore, stayed within his or her *'ohana,* knowing the family connections and bloodlines.

Many such adopted persons, now grown up, have beautiful and self-affirming memories of being raised by an auntie or *tutu* (grandmother), yet having an immediate family elsewhere who took interest in their upbringing. The special feeling those of Hawaiian descent have for their grandparents results in part from the tradition of *hanai*. A few others have painful memories of being sent away from home and siblings to be raised by relatives.

HAOLE • A Caucasian.

Originally, *haole* referred to any outsider but, with the coming of many races during the late nineteenth and early twentieth centuries, many of them with darker skins and working side by side at hard labor with little pay, the term was gradually narrowed to mean only whites.

According to one mistaken etymology, the word comes from the combination of *ha* or breath and *'ole* or without and means "without breath." This is another way of saying "people who lack the vital breath of life."

Haole can carry many connotations, depending on circumstances. In a jestful interchange between friends and in many racial jokes told in the Islands, it has no negative overtones whatever. It simply acknowledges Hawaii's racial variety and, if anything, conveys acceptance of everyone's differences. In less friendly exchanges, it can be used as an insult, just as can other racial labels such as Pordagee, **Pake**, or **Kotonk**.

Stereotypes of the *haole* differ widely, too. To some, *haole* conveys an image of pushy, cocky, materialistic people with a selfish, colorless lifestyle. To others, it conveys intelligence, efficiency, practicality, and know-how.

HAPA HAOLE

A person who is part white (part *haole*).

HAWAII PONO'I

This official state song was, like "Aloha Oe," written by royalty. In 1874 the "Merrie Monarch," King Kalakaua, composed lyrics that were then set to music by his royal bandmaster. It served briefly as the national anthem of the Kingdom of Hawaii until the overthrow and annexation in the 1890s. In 1967 it once again was given official status when the legislature declared it the state song. The words admonish the people to look to their leaders, their founders, and their children, and to do their duty.

Hawaii pono'i	(Hawaii's own people,)
Nana i kou mo'i	(Look to your king,)
Ka lani ali'i	(Your royal leader,)
Ke ali'i	(Your chief.)
Makua lani e	(Noble ancestor)
Kamehameha e	(Kamehameha,)
Na kaua e pale	(We will fight and defend)
Me ka ihe	(With the spear.)
Hawaii pono'i	(Hawaii's own people,)
Nana i na ali'i	(Look to your chiefs,)
Na pua muli kou	(And so teach the children after you,)
Na poki'i	(The younger ones.)
Hawaii pono'i	(Hawaii's own,)
E ka lahui e	(O nation,)
'O kau hana nui	(Think of your great duty.)
E ui e	(Seek guidance.)

HAWAIIAN • See NATIVE HAWAIIAN.

HAWAIIAN HOMESTEADS

An act of Congress in 1921 called the Hawaiian Homes Act set aside 189,000 acres of land for homesteading, farming, and ranching by **native Hawaiians**. The Act was well intended, but much of the land was substandard for use in agriculture. Nor has the administration of the terms of the Act satisfied many of those who should benefit from it. Currently, only about 6,000 people of Hawaiian ancestry have received homestead allotments, while 19,000 applicants are still waiting.

Leases are for 99 years, renewable for another 100. To qualify for a homestead, a person must have at least 50 percent Hawaiian blood. Leases may be passed on to relatives with at least 25 percent Hawaiian blood.

HAWAIIAN LANGUAGE

Hawaiian words like *aloha, haole, kokua*, and *pau* are so pervasive that one might conclude that the Hawaiian language lives in good health in the rural valleys of the Islands. This view is far from correct. The Hawaiian language is dangerously close to extinction as a medium of everyday communication. Within a few decades, it may live on only in academic study.

It is estimated that only 2,000 speakers of Hawaiian remain today, mostly older people. The group on which the survival of the language depends—young children—is frightfully small. Only about 30 youngsters under the age of five speak conversational Hawaiian, and only on Ni'ihau can one find small clusters of families who speak it at home. Because language carries the subtle nuances and patterns of thinking we call "culture," the death of the Hawaiian language may also mark the death of an integrated and whole way of life.

The threat of extinction of their language alarms the custodians of Hawaiian culture. But they differ in their vision of what can be done. Several educators have organized preschools in which children learn Hawaiian; others pressure the Department of Education to make Hawaiian a more important part of the general curriculum. Yet others see these measures as futile, arguing that until the same social and economic incentives that exist for learning English or pidgin apply to learning Hawaiian, the language may be learned but never used. And use is the key to the language's healthy survival.

Other peoples have brought nearly extinct languages back to life. These include Welsh in Great Britain and Navajo in North America. Hebrew had ceased to be a living language when it was decreed the language of modern Israel. Whether Hawaiians can produce the same results will depend largely on the kind of determination they bring to bear on the task. At present, the prospects are not hopeful.

On Sunday evenings, radio station KCCN broadcasts the only Hawaiian-language radio program in the world, *"Kaleo O Hawaii,"* featuring interviews and commentary.

However, knowledge of a few basic Hawaiian words is as necessary as a towel to a beach trip. For a survival list of Hawaiian words and clues on pronunciation, consult the **Glossaries** near the end of the book.

HEIAU

The *heiau* or Hawaiian temple was a place of great power and reverence. Ruins of *heiau* are scattered throughout the Islands and can be visited today. Respectful locals often leave a small lava rock wrapped in a *ti* leaf along the perimeter. *Heiau* were constructed with sturdy lava rock walls enclosing flat grounds covered with smooth stones or pebbles. Within the walls, altars, platforms for images and rituals, oracle towers, and small buildings for holding artifacts were constructed as needed.

Temples served different purposes. The most awesome were the *heiau luakini*, built by the highest chiefs and used for human sacrifice. More benign were the *heiau ho'ola* or healing temples, where priests of medicinal arts functioned, and the *pu'uhonua* or place of refuge, where fugitives, criminals, and those under penalty for breaking *kapu* could find sanctuary.

HOLOKU GOWN

Worn on elegant and formal occasions, the *holoku* gown is an adaptation of the full-length dress worn by the wives of missionaries who arrived in Hawaii starting in 1820. Apparently its name derived from the exclamations of Hawaiian women on first seeing the full, long, and straight skirts draping from sleeved bodices. *Holo*! means "run," and *ku*! means "stand." In other words, here is clothing we can walk and stand in with ease. However questionable this word history, the gown, with and without train, has remained a feature of island fashion.

The *holoku* achieved early popularity and retained it partly because it accommodated the fuller figure of Hawaii's women. In 1907, a reporter wrote in the *Hawaiian Gazette*, "The missionaries with their good, hard New

England sense, at once perceived that tight bodices and belts were unsuited to the figures of their new friends, to say nothing of not being adapted to the climate, so they invented a garment, cool, flowing and graceful—the holoku."

HUI

In a general sense, the Hawaiian word *hui* means club, association, or organization. Similarly, "to *hui*" means to meet or join together.

But often this term has financial implications. Because of the low income of many immigrants who worked on plantations or in service jobs, few had the resources to invest or start a business on their own. Therefore, those who wanted to do so organized *hui* to pool resources and make investment possible. The term then began to refer to more general types of partnerships or economic associations.

HULA

"Keep your eyes on the hands" goes the refrain to a popular *hula* number performed for tourists. The message conveyed is (1) the hands tell the story and (2) if you watch the hands, you won't be aroused by the beautiful figure and swaying hips. Both story and alluring movement are authentic parts of *hula*. But how closely do the numbers seen at night clubs and Polynesian revues resemble the authentic dance of ancient Hawaii? More closely than they did thirty years ago, thanks to the Hawaiian Renaissance of the sixties and the revival of men's *hula*.

Legends vary as to how *hula* originated. The most common refers to two mythical figures, Laka and Hopoe, who brought the dance to Hawaii and imparted it to selected people, who gradually varied it and protected it with restrictions. In pre-contact Hawaii, *hula* was a sacred dance performed on special occasions by highly trained and disciplined dancers. But as in all Polynesian societies, dance was also a part of community life for everyone. Part of what we consider *hula* today no doubt descends from dances commoners would perform.

Those selected for training had often distinguished themselves for beauty and grace of movement and studied under a master—a ***kumu hula***—in a ***halau*** or school. The training was rigorous and governed by *kapu*. Tradition points to the selection of women to *halau*, but scholars suggest that the earliest forms of *hula* were male dances instigated by the god Laka and eventually taught to women. Early drawings of Hawaii show dancing men arrayed in anklets and other ornaments. These dances, at once sacred and erotic, were performed to chants addressed to or in behalf of the gods. The erotic movements were meant to attract the gods' attention and interest them in the affairs of humans.

Had it not been for King Kalakaua, the *hula* might have been lost completely. Missionaries succeeded in banning its performance because of its sexual appeal. During the mid-nineteenth century it survived publicly only in cheap *hulahula* shows performed for sailors by less than well-trained dancers. Legitimate dancers and masters of the *hula* had to keep their knowledge and skills to themselves in hope that they could pass on their expertise before they died. That day came in the 1880s, when King Kalakaua ordered the dance to be performed on public occasions.

When the *hula* reappeared, it had changed. Much of the religion of Hawaii had been lost, so the dance had shed many of its sacred associations. And the erotic element was toned down considerably, although one can still see vestiges of suggestive movement in the ancient style *hula* performed today.

Two branches of *hula* exist. The *hula kahiko* or ancient-style *hula* is performed to chants and the rhythmic pounding and slapping of three types of rhythm instruments: the *ipu hula* or two gourds glued together, the *pahu hula* or shark skin drum, and the *'uli 'uli* or *'ulili* or double and triple gourd rattles. It is an energetic, pulsating dance full of simple, bold movement. Costuming usually approximates the ancient dress: men wear the *malo* or short wrap-around, with ti leaf anklets and headwear, and women, the longer wrap-around. Dances tell of legends, but the movements conveying meaning are less elaborate than in modern *hula*. Few dance performances in the world can surpass the energy and thrill brought about by a well-trained group performing *hula kahiko*.

The other type, *hula 'auana*, is the type most people outside Hawaii picture when they hear the term *hula*. It is the modern variety, mixing traditional footwork with more varied and soft body movement and gesture, and performed to music and songs (*'auana* means to drift or wander). Modern *hula* numbers can range from those performed in grass skirts to formal solo numbers performed in a ***holoku*** gown. Grass skirts, incidentally, are not authentic, but an import from the Gilbert Islands.

Men's *hula* is now very common, but it came close to disappearing. *Hula* troupes after Kalakaua's time did not include men, even though teachers remembered dances specifically for men and could remember seeing men perform. As *hula* emerged again, men's *hula* was relegated to the status of a comedy act, often with effeminate overtones. In the 1960s several *hula* teachers began to recover the lost art of men's *hula*. They drew on the knowledge of old *hula* masters and their observations of dance in other Polynesian societies to encourage groups of young Hawaiian men to perform ancient-style *hula* with movements appropriate for men. The form soon spread to other troupes and is now standard.

Ancient or modern, all *hula* numbers tell stories. Some recount ancient legends of lovers or of gods; others praise the beauty of a person or a place of special meaning. In most cases, however, *hula* numbers include a surface or straightforward meaning and a *ka 'ano* or hidden meaning. For example, a traditional number performed to an old song may on the surface describe the beauty of Oahu, but its imagery may also allude to scandals surrounding the royal family.

Hula numbers can vary almost infinitely, but nearly all of them are composed using a small number of basic steps and movements. A few of these basic steps are the *ami* or hip circle, in which the hips rotate as the dancer also rotates completely around; the *o'ehe* or knee lift, in which the dancer thrusts the knees apart with the legs bent; the vamp or *ka holo*, in which the dancer takes four steps to one side and four back to the other, usually with the lead hand extended; and the *hela* or toe point, in which the dancer alternates pointing right and left feet from a bent-leg position.

The premier *hula* competition at present, the Merrie Monarch Festival, held in April in Hilo each year, honors by its name the king who restored *hula* to Hawaiian life. Other important *hula* festivals are the King Kamehameha Hula and Chant Competition, held at the Neal Blaisdell Center Arena in Honolulu in June, and the Prince Lot Hula Festival, held at Moanalua Gardens in Honolulu in July.

HULA HALAU

A *halau* is a school; a *hula halau* is a school for teaching *hula*. When one joins a *halau*, one is not simply signing up for a class at a community college. One can take classes through a *halau*, but joining one is another matter. For the ***kumu hula*** and many students, the *halau* is their most intimate contact with the Hawaiian cultural heritage. Consequently, many *halau* try to instill a spirit of ***'ohana*** and teach Hawaiian religion and customs. The many hours of rehearsal, together with the pressures of performance and competition, make *halau* relationships intense and personal.

Halau compete in *hula* festivals and competitions. Therefore, each *halau* may strive to develop a style that sets it slightly apart from others. Tension exists between the need to preserve traditional steps, movements, and costuming and the need for creativity and development of the art. Audiences erupt with applause and cheers when they see a familiar number executed with exacting precision, as well as when they see a slight but brilliant innovation in dress or movement.

IMU

The *imu*, an underground oven, is a style of cooking that, like barbecue, lends its own unique and delicious flavor to food. It is time-consuming and labor-intensive, but the results "goin broke da mout, for sure." The combination of juices from meats, mild smoke, steam, and heat from the rocks in the oven bring out a taste that is to the mouth what a rainbow over the ocean is to the eyes.

To make an *imu*, the cooks first dig a deep pit, and in it they make a blazing fire, preferably of *kiawe* wood. When the fire is raging, lava rocks (other kinds don't work because they shatter from the heat) are placed in the pit and heated to hundreds of degrees. As the fire dies down, the coals are removed or brushed away, and the rocks are spread out. The cooks place cut banana stumps as the first layer to provide steam and prevent the food from burning on the hot rocks. Then they line the oven with banana leaves and on them place a pig stuffed with hot rocks and wrapped in its own banana leaves. Around the pig go sweet potatoes, *laulau*, fish, chicken, and anything else the cooks think will be tasty. They cover the food with more leaves and then place the last of the hot rocks over it, followed by a woven mat. Then they go do something else for a good part of the day as the hot rocks slowly do their work. At last, the pit is carefully uncovered and the food removed and prepared for eating.

This kind of cooking was strictly men's work in ancient Polynesia.

IPU

An *ipu* is a dry gourd of the bottle gourd variety used as a rhythm instrument to accompany chanting and dancing. An *ipu* can be made of a single gourd trained into a pear shape or from two gourds fastened together at the narrow end.

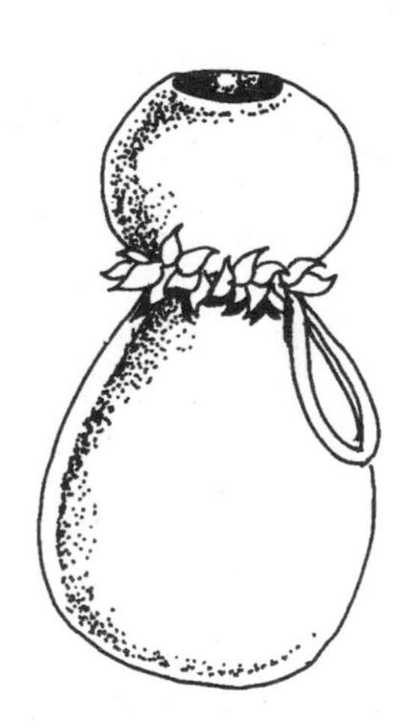

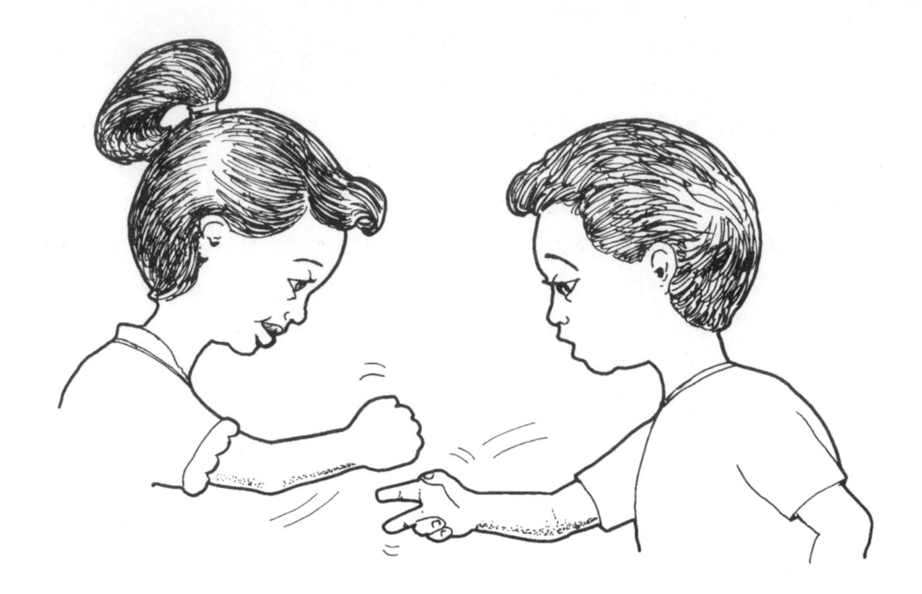

JUNK AN' A PO

Ever seen children play "paper, stone, and scissors" with their hands? *Junk an' a po* is the island version of this game, a revealing blend of Japanese words turned into pidgin and the hand signs of the similar American game, scissors, rock, and paper. The words to the game, "Junk an' a po, I canna show," are very similar in sound to those of the original Japanese, "*Jan Ken Po*" and "*Ai Kono Sho.*" In the Japanese game, players make signs with their fists and fingers representing frogs, slugs, and snakes. A frog beats a slug, a slug beats a snake, and a snake beats a frog. The game has been seen as a symbol of Hawaii's cultural mixing, in which ingredients become transformed into ways of seeing and behaving that stand on their own, incorporating the old patterns yet differing from them.

KA LAHUI HAWAII

Ka Lahui Hawaii is an organization of Hawaiians and supporters working to establish a sovereign nation of native Hawaiians in the Islands, fashioned along the lines of American Indian nations on the mainland. See **Native Hawaiian.**

KAHILI

At pageants and festivals, *kahili* standards often precede the festival court. These are long poles topped with drum-shaped ornaments of red and yellow feathers. In ancient times, *kahili* were carried before high chiefs and royalty to identify them and to warn commoners to make way by standing aside, sitting, or even lying down for very high chiefs.

KAHUNA

Hawaiian for priest or expert.

Fear them? Revere them? What attitude should one take toward those who practice the ancient arts of *kahuna*-ism? That question you will have to answer for yourself. It will help you to know something of the history of the *kahuna* and how the traditions are kept alive today.

In ancient Hawaii there were many kinds of *kahuna*. Any expert in an art or craft was considered a *kahuna,* as were priests and sorcerers. Two kinds that survive today are the *kahuna lapa'au* or the healer skilled in herbs and the lore of curing, and the *kahuna 'ana'ana* or the sorcerer skilled in chants and charms that influence the good and evil forces of life. A third type of *kahuna* may combine arts of the two just mentioned, but primarily dedicates his or her energy to the preservation of a ***heiau*** or the worship of a particular god.

For many decades *kahuna* were forced to practice their knowledge and rituals in secret. In 1819, King Kamehameha II abolished the ***kapu*** system, with its complex network of religion and behavior restrictions. The place of the *kahuna* as priest and enforcer of the system quickly weakened. The following year Christian missionaries arrived in Hawaii, depicting Hawaiian religion as a force of evil and darkness. Since then, it is difficult to know who the *kahuna* are and what sort of arts they have preserved, even in the "anything goes" atmosphere of the late twentieth century.

Some *kahuna* are well known. Momi Mo'okini Lum stands in a direct line of practicing *kahuna* going back over fifteen generations. She serves as a *kahuna nui* or high priestess of the *Mo'okini Luakini*—a *heiau* in the Kohala District of the Big Island—where she disseminates knowledge of the *heiau* and Hawaiian religion. Morrnah Nalamaku

Simeona is a practicing *kahuna lapa'au* who combines Hawaiian healing arts with contemporary knowledge to teach people how to resolve problems and relieve stress. Lanakila Brandt practices the *kahuna* arts on the Big Island, where he retired after an entertainment career on Oahu. Brandt was selected by his grandfather to learn the extensive knowledge of the *kahuna* while still a boy.(14)

But most *kahuna* share their ways with only a selected few. They don't even organize or communicate regularly among themselves. Since the *kahuna* arts were passed down within single families when it was not prudent to use the arts openly, each *kahuna* may have a distinctive view of the whole; each has, as it were, a group of strands of the myriad once woven into Hawaiian life. To pool these distinctive arts would be, to many *kahuna*, to weaken, and possibly lose, the strands held sacred by the individual *kahuna*.

Nevertheless, the *kahuna* has an important place in the public life of Hawaii. Dedications of public buildings (and many large structures in the private sector) rarely take place without a *kahuna's* blessing. After bad luck or mishaps in a construction project, a supervisor may invite a *kahuna* to appease or neutralize hostile spirits.

How do the *kahuna* reconcile their arts with the religions of modern Hawaii? In as many ways as there are *kahuna*. A few look upon Christianity as an intrusion—an unwelcome but firmly established foreign influence. Others take part in Christian worship without feeling any inner conflict. They see both sides as different but harmonious manifestations of a spiritual order to life, an order that human minds cannot reduce to rational systems.

Even among those of Hawaiian ancestry, attitudes toward *kahuna*-ism differ. Some families stay strictly away from it as from a force that is real but too dangerous to handle. Others quietly go about the business of selecting heirs and passing on their knowledge. Very few dismiss the *kahuna* as irrelevant or powerless.

KAI

Kai is Hawaiian for ocean or ocean water. *Kai* is used in creating many place names (e.g., Hawaii Kai), as well as in the directional word *makai*—toward the sea. Caution: in some Polynesian languages it is an offensive word.

KAMA'AINA

A *Kama'aina* is a long-time resident of the Islands who knows the local ways. Literally, a *kama'aina* is a "child of the land"—or, in other words, someone born in Hawaii; but the term is more frequently used to refer to someone who moved here and has stayed long enough to fit in.

A *kama'aina* considers Hawaii home, even though he or she may also be "from" somewhere else. Such a person accepts the people of Hawaii and feels a common bond with them, even though their customs at home may differ. A *kama'aina* doesn't necessarily talk pidgin and doesn't necessarily have a big wardrobe of *aloha* shirts or *muumuus.* He or she knows that parading a few expressions in pidgin may mark one as trying too hard and mask one's true identity. But the *kama'aina* does know the subcurrent of local ways: knows when to buy Portuguese sausage or sweet bread from a neighbor kid, and when to help sell it to benefit an organization; knows when it's okay to drop in at a *lu'au* without being invited; knows when to bring food to a social gathering (nearly always); knows a good plate lunch and a good many local food favorites; knows how to give respect to others and avoid stepping on toes, even in swapping ethnic jokes.

No minimum length of time qualifies one as *kama'aina*, and no one officially confers the status. It comes gradually, with the right attitudes.

For some colorful contrasts between *kama'aina* and *malihini* (newcomer), see ***malihini***.

KAMEHAMEHA DAY

A state holiday on June 11 honors King Kamehameha the Great, the first ruler to extend sway over all the islands of Hawaii. Kamehameha came from the Kohala district of the Big Island. His unification of the Islands took place in 1805, when he formed a treaty with the ruling chief of Kauai after conquering the other islands.

Kamehameha Day is celebrated with a parade and a street party in Honolulu. One important tradition is the draping of the Kamehameha Statue in front of the State Judiciary Building in downtown Honolulu with *leis* and floral wreaths.

KANAKA

In the Hawaiian language: a person, a human. In today's use, however, it has come to signify a Hawaiian man or boy.

KAPU

Kapu means taboo, forbidden. Like many Hawaiian terms, this one is used in different senses. A *kapu* sign on a piece of property means only "keep out." But in the older sense, it applies to behavior that is forbidden. More broadly still, the *kapu* system was a way of regulating daily routines and conducting relationships within the prescribed limits for each sex and class.

A historian writes that the *kapu* system was:

> highly developed in Polynesia and common among primitive peoples throughout the world. The system provided a religious sanction for the daily rules of life and for the structure of both society and government. In essence it proceeded from the Polynesian view that some parts of nature are sacred (including the masculine principle and life), and that some are profane (including the feminine principle and death). Some *kapus* were permanent. There were several sacred days each month for religious rituals. A commoner was forbidden to stand in the presence of a chief. Women were forbidden to eat pork, bananas, and some kinds of fish. They had to cook their food separately and eat apart from their male masters. In addition to these permanent prohibitions, the chiefs and priests occa-

> sionally imposed special *kapus*. . . Many abuses resulted. The penalty for violating a *kapu* could be severe. A death sentence was not unusual, even if the offender had unknowingly broken one of the sacred rules. An amusing survival of this often cruel system appears in the many *kapu* signs posted as "no trespassing" warnings throughout the Islands today.
>
> The *kapu* system was part of the general Hawaiian religion of nature worship. Each important act, such as building a house or preparing for war, had its own special rites.(15)

The *kapu* system was officially abolished in 1819 by King Kamehameha II. The King could see that the *kapu* system was an obstacle between his people and the apparently better organized and equipped outsiders. Unfortunately, there was no equivalent system ready to replace it, so the Hawaiian people were left culturally adrift, cut off from their old ways without an appropriate substitute to help them make the transition into the modern world.

KAUKAU

Pidgin for "food" or "eat."

This is not a Hawaiian language term.

KEIKI • Child, offspring.

This term has affectionate overtones. Sometimes it refers to nonhuman things. For example, the young banana plants growing around a mature stock are called *keiki.*

KEN CLUBS

The term *Ken* clubs comes from the Japanese word *kenjinkai*, meaning "prefectural association." A prefecture is a local government unit in Japan, similar to a county. *Ken* clubs are associations of Japanese-Americans in Hawaii descending from ancestors in designated locales or prefectures in Japan. For example, the *Shinyu Aloha Kai* gathers those whose grandparents came from Hiroshima. One *ken* club admits any Japanese-American who is a college graduate.

KEN PICNICS

Ken picnics are sponsored by and for members of *ken* clubs. On Oahu, *ken* picnics are often held during the summer at Ala Moana Beach Park.

Ken picnics offer a rare opportunity to observe Japanese-American traditions, to see different generations interacting—the *issei, nisei, sansei,* and *yonsei*—and to observe the interplay of Japanese, American, and local customs. Food, games, music—all exhibit the incorporation of old and new and represent the distinct identity of the Japanese in Hawaii.

KOA

A native hardwood (*Acacia koa*) of dark finish is used in making furniture, bowls, and other decorative objects. It has been called the Hawaiian mahogany. *Koa* trees can grow up to 70 feet in height. In ancient Hawaii, *koa* wood made excellent canoe hulls, paddles, clubs, bowls, and utensils. Stands of *koa* are found on the Big Island. Unsuccessful attempts have been made to grow it outside of Hawaii.

KONA

Kona is a district on the leeward (west) side of the Big Island.

KONA WINDS

Winds from out of the south are called Kona winds. Unlike Hawaii's prevailing trade winds, Kona winds blow warm and dry, brushing the south and leeward sides first. With Hawaii's humidity, that means muggy, sticky heat. Kona winds usually don't last more than a week, so, when they arrive, dress cool and endure.

KOREAN BAR

This term is something of a misnomer. It is used to refer to a "hostess bar," a drinking establishment in which women who work on the premises will offer their company (and sometimes more) in return for drinks purchased for them. Their drinks cost $10 to $20 and are usually nothing more than weak tea with a small amount of alcohol to make them smell like the real thing.

If you want to go to a Korean Bar, have a clear head about what you want and how much you're willing to spend. Some hostesses are expert wheedlers and will read you better than a psychologist can.

KOTONK • A mainland Japanese

Kotonk is not quite a neutral term, though it can be used in good humor among friends. The origins of the name are cloudy; almost all versions reveal prejudice in favor of the local Japanese and against their mainland counterparts. One theory holds *kotonk* to be the sound a coconut makes bouncing off the head of a mainland Japanese American. In other words, the newly arrived mainland Japanese is too naive (or stupid) to avoid falling coconuts. (In fact, even Polynesians of the South Pacific are occasionally injured by falling coconuts.) Another derogatory theory holds that *kotonk* is the sound made when the head of a mainland Japanese hits the floor, after being punched by a local.

KUHIO DAY

This state holiday commemorates the life of Prince Jonah Kuhio Kalanianaole. A member of the royal family, Prince Kuhio was elected to the U. S. Congress in 1902, shortly after the overthrow of the monarchy and annexation of Hawaii. He served until 1922. Kuhio's status as royal prince and elected official led to his being called the "Citizen Prince."

KUKUI • The candlenut tree, or the nut of that tree.

The *kukui* is the state tree, having replaced the coconut palm in that capacity in 1959. In ancient Hawaii, the *kukui* tree and nut had many uses. The nut was cracked and its oil burned for light; the plant was therefore revered as a source of light. Its oil was used to anoint infants. Its wood was used to carve the pig head symbols marking the boundaries between *ahupua'a* or land divisions. Fishermen chewed the nut and spit its oily residue on the water to create a film through which they could more clearly see fish. The *kukui* also had medicinal uses. Today, *leis* are made of the nuts, polished to a dark luster.

KULEANA

"That's not my *kuleana,*" people say, even on the mainland. In this usage *kuleana* means "area of responsibility." In Hawaii, however, *kuleana* has a much more specific meaning from which the one above derives. A *kuleana* is a parcel of fee-simple property belonging to a family and originally recognized back in 1855 by the Kingdom of Hawaii Land Commission. This commission oversaw the awarding of deeds after the Great *Mahele,* or great land division. Lands were divided among the king, chiefs, and commoners. Commoners who could show they had in fact been working a parcel of land could be awarded title to it.

In some parts of the Islands, irregular *kuleana* break up the otherwise geometric property lines, much to the irritation of developers and large landholders who wish the owners would sell. To the Hawaiian families who own them, *kuleana* represent a link with the land and with a time when their ancestors worked it in the old way, belonging to it, not having it belong to them.

KUMU HULA

A hula master; a leader of a
hula halau.

One can't take a state examination to be licensed as a *hula* master. The process consists of an apprenticeship under an acknowledged artist. In some cases, a promising pupil is asked by a master to become a protege. When the apprentice has learned to the point of mastery, he or she assumes the name of *kumu hula* and may set up a *hula halau.* This process may seem unregulated, but there is a kind of self-check built in. Initially, a new *kumu hula* may attract little attention from established masters. However, by performing at festivals and winning prizes at *hula* competitions, the young master gains recognition and eventually joins the ranks of respected experts.

KUMULIPO

Generally, this is a birth or genealogy chant, but it is also the title of a specific Hawaiian creation chant, composed around the mid-1700s for Chief Ka limamao to recite his ancestry and recount myths of the origins of life. One of the greatest creation chants to be preserved from pre-contact Hawaii, it was originally translated into English by Queen Lili'uokalani and published in 1897. Several more recent translations are available by Martha Beckwith, Theodore Kelsey, and Rubellite Kawena Johnson.

The 2,000 line poem describes life originating in the slime and slowly arising from the simplest forms such as the coral polyp and marine invertebrates (worms, urchins, shellfish, etc.) to the more complex plants, insects, birds, mammals, and, finally, humans. The poem has attracted the attention of historians of science because it gives a naturalistic, nondivine account of the creation of life forms drawn from close observation and thus coincides roughly with the evolutionary theories of Darwin that appeared over a century after its composition.

KUPUNA • Grandparent.

The term today refers to an elderly member of the family or an older teacher. If you have elementary school age children, you will likely hear them refer to older people who teach them Hawaiian customs and crafts as *kupuna*.

In traditional Hawaiian culture, the senior elders or *hanau mua* received great respect and were relied on for wisdom and counsel. In Hawaii today, few families make clear distinctions of "senior eldest," but they do rely on elder members of the family for help in solving problems.

LAVALAVA

A single piece of fabric wrapped around the body as a garment, the *lavalava* is one of the most versatile pieces of clothing you will ever wear. It can serve as a beach wrap, a bathrobe, an outer garment for informal occasions outside, a ground cloth, and so on. Many who learn to throw one around their waist in Hawaii take their *lavalava* when they move away.

The *lavalava* can be purchased just about anywhere local crafts are sold. Incidentally, it makes an excellent gift to newcomers. It is not a Hawaiian article of dress, but came from the South Pacific.

LEI • A flower necklace.

No other object of Hawaiian culture can rival the *lei* as a symbol of welcome, floral beauty, and *aloha*. *Leis* are made from numerous types of flower blossoms that grow in Hawaii, as well as from plants or plant parts. The coveted *maile lei* is made from the leaves and stems of the *maile* plant. The *ti lei* is woven from strands of *ti* leaf. The *hala lei* strings together the small, dry, brush-like segments of the fruit of the *hala* or *pandanus* tree. *Leis* are also strung from *kukui* nuts, shells, and—let's not forget the children's favorites—candy, **crack seed**, or money. The most common flower *leis* are made from plumeria, the purple Vanda orchid, carnation, *pua*, or crown flowers.

The *lei* custom brings together floral beauty and Hawaiian love and respect:

> In the Hawaiian culture, a person's head and shoulders are considered sacred parts of the body, to be respected by others. Honoring those who are loved and respected has always been a fundamental value in Hawaii. It appears natural, when

considering these cultural values, that the placing of a lei over the head and around the shoulders of a person would exemplify the bestowing of honor and respect.(16)

Curiously, the use of strung flower *leis* can't be documented in pre-contact Hawaii. In ancient Hawaii, *lei wili* (twisted *leis* made from fragrant leaves) and feather *leis* predominated. Legends associate the *maile lei* with the goddess of *hula*, but the tradition is difficult to verify. The earliest records or photos of floral *leis* show twisted vines with a few blossoms woven in. It should also be noted that the Hawaii of two hundred years ago did not offer the variety of plants and flowers seen today. So the flower *lei* has apparently blossomed as a part of modern Hawaii.

Leis can be classified into four types: *lei kui* or string *lei*, the *lei haku* or open-ended *lei* woven or braided on a backing, the *lei wili* or braided or twisted *lei* with no backing material, and the *lei hipu'u* or knotted *lei*. Strung *leis* are made using a *lei* needle (a long steel needle available in many local stores) and thread (No. 10 cotton thread is recommended). Directions with photographs for making *leis* using different blossoms and plant material can be found in *Hawaiian Flower Lei Making* by Adren and Josephine Bird.

When selecting a *lei*, let your feeling for the person and occasion guide you. There does not seem to be any rule associating different flower *leis* with specific occasions or gender. In fact, any occasion is a good occasion for a *lei*, including those days when you feel like giving one for no specific reason at all. The *maile lei*, a twisted *lei* made from the leaves and vine of the *maile* plant, has special status among those of Hawaiian ancestry and is given to older or particularly close people. It is often seen at weddings, graduations, and election victory celebrations. It is also used in opening ceremonies for new buildings. On the latter occasion, it should not be cut, but merely knotted and then untied or gathered aside. Probably the premier occasion for observing *leis* is a high-school or college graduation. There you will see *leis* stacked so high on the shoulders of graduates that they can barely see out.

It is considered bad form to wear a *lei* that you have made or bought for someone else. Locals of a more traditional bent view this as similar to buying someone a piece of clothing and wearing it first. Better to keep it in a bag or wear it over the arm until time to bestow it. However, once a person has received a *lei* and worn it, that person may in turn place the *lei* on someone else. When people give a *lei* to someone of the opposite sex, they usually accompany the *lei* with a kiss on the cheek.

Leis will stay fresh longer if they are kept in a plastic bag in the refrigerator.

LEI DAY

Lei Day is a celebration held May 1 with exhibits and *lei*-making competitions at Kapiolani Park in Honolulu.

LILIKOI • Hawaiian name for passion fruit.

Lilikoi can be gathered in many of the valleys and hillsides of the Islands, particularly in areas with frequent rain. It makes excellent jam and juice. The flavor is extracted by removing the seed and pulp from inside the thick skin and then crushing or straining them.

LION DANCE

At festivals and special events involving the Chinese, you are likely to witness a dance using a large stylized lion head with long, colorful, flowing material for its body. It takes a team of people to keep the lion moving—one to hold up the head and from two to six to perform as the body.

The lion symbolizes wealth and long life. Legend has it that the gods assigned the courageous lion to guard the fruit of immortality. The

lion dance often depicts attempts to steal the fruit. First, as the lion rests, a warrior sneaks up and tries to carry off the fruit, but the lion rouses itself to confront the warrior. As the lion returns to rest, a crafty monk approaches, distracts the lion, and makes off with the fruit. The lion gives chase but eventually is won over to admire the monk's intelligence.

LI-SEE

On special occasions, many Chinese give money wrapped in red paper or placed in a red envelope. Money given in this way brings luck. Some shops sell red envelopes with designs printed on them. Each design conveys a wish for the recipient: peaches for longevity, fish for bountiful times, bamboo for peace, coins for wealth, and so forth.

LU'AU • Feast.

The *lu'au* features in every newcomer's vision of life in Hawaii. What the newcomer may not know, especially if his or her only *lu'au* is a packaged event for tourists, is the extent of generosity involved in hosting one. The family down the street with a son graduating from high school or daughter getting married can spend a month's income buying food. Accept your plate of pork, rice, raw fish, *taro*, sweet potato, long rice, and cake in the spirit in which it is given. And be aware that a *lu'au* is not just a big feed or a corporate function to drift in and out of without making yourself known. Always greet the hosts. Thank them and give congratulations if someone is being honored.

A *lu'au* is a celebration of love, family ties, and abundance. Neighbors and extended family share in cooking, setting up tarps and tables and chairs, lining up entertainment, and serving food. Just as the host family shares its resources to the stretching point, so do neighbors, friends, and family share in the accomplishments or special event in the life of the person being honored.

Most *lu'aus* serve some combination of roasted pork (called *kalua* pig if it's cooked in an ***imu*** or underground oven), chicken, long rice (clear rice noodles seasoned with ginger and served with chicken), steamed *taro, poi* (pounded *taro* paste, sometimes fermented), *ulu* (breadfruit), *poke* (raw fish seasoned with seaweed), *lomilomi* salmon (fish marinated with onions and tomatoes), *laulau* (a small bundle of food made of varying combinations of pork, beef, fish, and *taro,* all wrapped in *ti* leaves and cooked in the *imu*), and *haupia* (sweet coconut pudding).

Some words on *lu'au* etiquette. It is okay to drop in uninvited if you're a good friend of the host family. Occasionally, invitations (written or oral) don't get to everyone. If you feel close to the hosts, drop in anyway. If you're very close friends, make a joke about it: "Hey, we didn't get invited, but we couldn't miss it anyway." If the *lu'au* honors a person graduating or getting married or having a birthday, a card with money makes an appropriate (but not mandatory) gift.

For a family-type *lu'au*, casual *aloha* attire is always appropriate. An evening *lu'au* may call for *muumuus* for the women, dress pants and *aloha* shirts for men.

Unless entertainment has been extensively planned, you might want to be mentally prepared to be pulled up to the front to take part in a dance or song. It may happen only rarely, but it does happen. If so, smile and participate in good fun. And don't be annoyed on any account if it seems that others are having a little fun at your expense. Join in with a chuckle and consider it your return for the friendship and generosity of the hosts.

MAKAHIKI

When we say "party on!" we mean for a day or so. The ancient Hawaiians taught us the real meaning. For the four-month period starting in late October or early November, life changed dramatically. This was the time of the annual *Makahiki* Festival, a time of celebration looking forward to the return of the god Lono. Lono had sailed from Hawaii, distraught after having killed his wife in a fit of jealousy but promising to come back with an entire island abounding in food.

The festival was a time of rest during which nearly all activity took on a sacred character. It also coincided with a period of harvest and the start of the rainy season. *Makahiki,* therefore, meant plenty, peace, rain, and enjoyment of physical prowess. During the festival time, some ***kapu*** on foods and social interactions were removed, while others of a special kind were imposed. Led by the priests and *ali'i*, the people held long, ceremonial processions around the island; staged mock battles; collected taxes to be given to the paramount chief; held competitive games in boxing, wrestling, spear throwing, and so forth; and enforced special *kapu*. One of the most unusual was a ban on warfare. All fighting had to cease until the end of the festival.

In modern Hawaii, art festivals, sports festivals, Boy Scout demonstrations, and other kinds of celebrations still use the *makahiki* name.

MALIHINI • A newcomer.

If the terms fits, wear it. If you stay long enough, you will cease to be *malihini* and become *kama'aina*. No fixed length of stay confers the change in status; it is more a matter of becoming familiar with local ways and achieving a measure of self-identity as a resident of Hawaii. For some people, this can happen quickly.

The *Honolulu Magazine* printed a whimsical and useful list of items by which to distinguish *malihini* from *kama'aina*:

You're *malihini* if you . . .

- walk into a house with your shoes on
- think there's only one type of hula—the "Lovely Hula Hands" variety
- pronounce "Likelike" as "like-like"
- ask for a fork at a Japanese restaurant
- wear plastic *leis*
- think Longs Drugs is just a drug store
- take sandwiches on a picnic
- think May Day is an international labor celebration
- think women in *muumuus* are walking around in their nighties
- go to an event at Aloha Stadium and expect to find parking
- don't know the name of the city bus service
- wear a business suit even if you're not a lawyer or a sales clerk for Liberty House or Sears
- think "Banzai!" is a battle cry
- turn up your nose at *pupus*
- think "hana bata" is something to spread on toast
- wear socks with sandals
- call slippers "go-aheads" or "flip-flops"
- wear matching aloha attire with your mate
- think Iolani Palace is where the governor and Hawaii 5-0 have office
- call dinner "supper" and eat it at 9 p.m.
- call the mainland "stateside"
- think "bumbye" means a rotten deal or hobo sale
- think "mahalo" is the name of a trash receptacle.

You're *kama'aina* if you . . .

- can pronounce "Kalanianaole"

- have acquired a taste for crack seed
- say "shoyu" instead of "soy sauce"
- eat mangoes half-ripe with shoyu, sugar, and salt
- take rainbows for granted
- automatically take along a raincoat or umbrella when you go to Manoa
- say "shave ice" without the "d"
- eat *poi* without sugar
- have at least one baby *lu'au*
- know you shouldn't attempt to speak pidgin if you haven't grown up with it
- prefer guava jam and jelly over the Mainland stuff
- have a favorite beach that's not Waikiki
- know the difference between "sushi" and "shi-shi"
- see nothing wrong with having macaroni salad and two scoops of rice in your plate lunch
- pronounce "karate" and "sashimi" the right way (with the accent on the last syllables)
- wear baggy, puka T-shirts and shorts to bed at night
- refer to the Neal S. Blaisdell Center as "the H.I.C."
- buy your *leis* on Maunakea Street
- call an avocado a pear and eat it with sugar (and sometimes with shoyu)
- know that "Where's the beef?" has nothing to do with Wendy's hamburgers
- consider barefoot your favorite form of footwear
- catch a cold whenever trade winds change to kona winds
- know you should stay out of Waimea Bay when the surf is up
- understand all of Frank DeLima's songs and one-liners
- consider "pau" a complete sentence. (17)

MALO • A Hawaiian loin cloth, worn by men.

MANA

Mana is a Hawaiian term for personal spiritual power. In ancient Hawaii an elaborate system of social relations and restrictions protected the *mana* of the nobility and priests and, to a lesser extent, the commoners. Our culture today has little counterpart. Perhaps we can say *mana* is a combination of self-identity, an aura of power, and charisma. But it comes from supernatural sources, though it also passes naturally through inheritance and bloodlines. Many beliefs existed about how evil spirits, other people, or one's own self could rob a person of his or her *mana* and leave him or her exposed to other forces, cut off from protection, and powerless to act in the normal way. In Hawaii of today, the term *mana* can carry these connotations and is often used to refer to the gifts of the Holy Spirit, but generally you will hear it used to refer to control of oneself and one's destiny or to feeling comfortable and unthreatened.

MENEHUNE

Menehune are dark, mischievous race of dwarfs who, according to legend, lived in ancient Hawaii and were later displaced or eradicated after the arrival of Polynesian settlers.

Two versions of the *menehune* legend can be heard: that of local lore and that of the scholar. In local lore, the *menehune* were responsible for building a few surprising structures in early Hawaii, notably the "*menehune* ditch" on Kauai. *Menehune* were thought to have preceded the arrival of Hawaiians and to have been displaced eventually. Some locals, however, believe that the *menehune* still haunt the Islands and carry out tricks on inhabitants.

Then there is the scholar's view:

> . . . such legends [of clever dwarfs of a former age] existed in various islands of Melanesia and Micronesia and in other islands of the Polynesian triangle as well as in Hawaii. Apparently all these legends derive from a common substratum of mythology and are reinterpreted in terms of local conditions by various groups. Thus in Hawaii the ancient legends of mischievous and highly talented dwarfs were interpreted to refer to the lower classes, who were probably called *menehune* in the early periods of Hawaiian prehistory. To this day in Tahiti the cognate term *menehune* refers to people of the lower class. Therefore it is reasonable to suppose that the Tahitian settlers brought the term to Hawaii, where it was first applied only to the lower class but was subsequently extended and transferred to the mythical dwarfs as a slight to the lower classes. Later the term for the lower classes was altered to the present form *maka'ainana*, leaving *menehune* as applicable to the dwarfs alone. It is now certain that no black dwarfs ever lived in the Hawaiian Islands at any time.(18)

MERRIE MONARCH FESTIVAL

What the World Series is to baseball, the Merrie Monarch Festival is to *hula*. This annual *hula* competition, held in late March or April in Hilo, takes its name from King Kalakaua, the "merrie monarch" who in the 1880s revived *hula* dancing from the ban placed upon it by missionaries in the 1820s and later passed into law. Had it not been for Kalakaua, who ordered a group to organize and perform on official occasions, the beautiful *hula*, so much a part of the Hawaiian heritage, might have passed into oblivion.

The festival brings the leading *halau* of the Islands together for two days of performance. Both ancient and modern styles are featured. A panel of *hula* experts evaluates competing groups and awards top honors to the best.

MOCHI

Mochi is a Japanese and Chinese delicacy made from pounded rice and served in small cakes of various shapes and colors on holidays. Some cakes contain a sweet bean paste. Traditionally, individual households or small groups of people would make their own *mochi*. Most families now buy the cakes from confectionary shops.

To make *mochi*, a special rice is soaked, steamed, and then placed in a large wood or rock mortar where it is pounded with wooden mallets (weighing up to ten pounds) until the resulting paste is smooth and doughy. The paste is then divided into smaller batches and formed into smooth cakes and covered with a potato starch, which gives it a dry, white coating for easy handling.

The shapes and colors the Japanese give to *mochi* vary with the holiday. For New Year, the cakes are made round and smooth to represent the sun and the moon and also wholeness. The rounded edges further suggest harmony. On Japanese **Girls' Day** (March 3), diamond-shaped cakes called *hishi mochi* are served. The shape is believed to have come from the leaf of a plant that extended life, and the colors (white, pink, and green) stand for purity, vigor, and fertility. **Boys' Day** (May 5) calls for *kashiwa mochi*. Its half-moon shape is said to represent the helmet worn by *samurai* (and so, warriorlike strength) with a wrapping suggesting the oak leaf's endurance and protection.

Hawaii residents of Chinese descent also make *mochi* for their special days, including Chinese New Year. Their word for the large *mochi* cake, *nien-gao*, can be interpreted to mean "year high"; eating the cake is a way of wishing for a year lived on an elevated plane. The *nien-gao* is made by pounding the *mochi* rice with brown sugar and then forming it into a plate-size cake and steaming that for about eight hours.

MOKE

(Pronounced to rhyme with "coke.") A *moke* is a young tough guy who passes the time hanging around, talking story, drinking beer, maybe taking a drag on a joint of *pakalolo* or marijuana, fighting, etc. The old mainland term "hood" has similar connotations but lacks the local flavor—the grubby T-shirt and slippers, the total use of pidgin, and so on.

MO'OLELO

Mo'olelo means "story." The term usually refers to ancient tales or legends preserved in memory and passed down orally. They are distinguished from purely fictional tales, though the line between the two is often blurred in oral history. *Mo'olelo* may contain family stories, recitations of customs for occasions like birth and burial, procedures for doing something like building, historical tales, actions of the gods, and chants. People who have a store of *mo'olelo* will often recount them only during daylight. It's bad luck in the dark.

MUUMUU

A *muumuu* is a loose-fitting, "Mother Hubbard" style of dress consisting of a simple yoke with a high neckline and long flowing skirt with no gathered waist. You'll hear some purists pronounce this word in the authentic way—that is, with a glottal stop between the double "u" in each syllable "*mu`umu`u*"--but most people say it "moomoo." The Hawaiian word *mu`umu`u* means short or cut off, and the dress was probably named this because it lacks the bodice portion of standard dress design.

For decades the *muumuu* was considered okay only for around the house. Its move to an important position in island fashion is part of the history of Hawaii's garment industry. As that industry grew in the forties and fifties and began to promote its own floral patterns and designs, the old "nightgown" or "housedress" *muumuu* acquired new appeal. By the sixties, mainland fashion designers and magazines such as *Vogue* had noticed and featured the *muumuu.* Today, many of Hawaii's women own *muumuus,* and it's a sure bet that at least one of them has ribbon trim and white eyelet material on the bib.

NAMES—CHINESE

Many persons of Chinese ancestry have two middle initials. Why is this so? Chinese personal names usually consist of two characters in Chinese script. Together they name an object, event, or virtue to aid a child in achieving the family's hopes for its future. The sounds for each Chinese character are transliterated into English when Hawaii's Chinese give a name; each sound is usually abbreviated when a person writes out his or her name. Paul Kwok Hing (prosperous country) Lam will usually write his name Paul K. H. Lam. Some other typical combinations are Kam Lan (golden flower), Foo Lin (socially rich), and Mei Lin (beautiful lotus). The name combination given to each child results from careful selection among the possible virtues or qualities parents want a child to have. Traditionally, an elder family member of wisdom and insight has the honor of selecting the name. In Hawaii today, many families preserve the custom of bestowing a Chinese name but select it in the same way they choose an English one—by preference.

NAMES—HAWAIIAN

If you have children while living in Hawaii, chances are you will give them a Christian first name and a Hawaiian middle name. In doing so, you'll be following a Hawaiian tradition that has legal foundations, though these have generally been forgotten. In 1860, King Kamehameha IV signed a law requiring that, from that time forth, all children must be given a family name taken from the father and a Christian name as well. Many families responded by converting biblical names into Hawaiian sounds; others bestowed two names, one Hawaiian, one Christian. Surprisingly, this law was not withdrawn until 1967.

The proper Hawaiian way to give a name is to present the child to a family elder or *kupuna*, who selects a name from the natural environment, intuition as to the child's nature, or some other source, such as an ancestor or a dream.

Many seemingly Hawaiian names such as Keoki (George) are not true Hawaiian names, but adaptations of English sounds into Hawaiian. A more authentic alternative is to translate the meaning of a Christian name into its Hawaiian equivalent. George, for example, comes from the Latin for farmer. Its equivalent in Hawaiian is *Mahi'ai*. You can find the whole range of Christian names and Hawaiian translations, as well as more information on naming, in *The Hawaiian Name Book*, by Patrick Ka'ano'i and the late Robert Lokomaika'iokalani Snakenberg.

NANNY NANNY BOO BOO • A taunt used by children.

NARCISSUS FESTIVAL

The Chinese Chamber of Commerce sponsors this annual festival to preserve Chinese traditions and promote trade and interest in Chinatown. It is staged several weeks before Chinese New Year and includes lion dances, fireworks, a beauty pageant, and other demonstrations and trade activities.

The name "Narcissus Festival" was chosen as more appropriate to the varied goals of the festival than "Chinese New Year." The narcissus is a fragrant flower of the lily family that has been cultivated and treasured by the Chinese. It is sometimes called "Chinese sacred lily" and blossoms between November and March.

NATIVE HAWAIIAN

What is a native Hawaiian? The question deserves a simple answer, but political, economic, and social ramifications make a simple answer difficult. To start with the political implications, the Native Hawaiians occupy a position similar to that of Native American Indians who peopled a land (they never thought of owning it any more than the native Hawaiians) and governed themselves until another people "discovered" them, won "ownership" of their land, and placed a government over them. It is true that many Hawaiian people, including their own leaders, took active parts in creating the present system of land ownership and government, but that hardly makes the memory sweeter. So, from a political point of view, native Hawaiians are descendants of the people who lived in Hawaii and are still struggling to gather enough strength in numbers and voice to have control of their destiny.

One avenue that Hawaiian people have taken to gain more political control of their lives is the proposed creation of a Native Hawaiian Nation. This movement seeks to restore sovereignty and create a nation within a nation, much as American Indian tribes have formed their own governments to rule their own lands and people. The United States government recognizes over three hundred such Indian nations that follow their own tribal laws and councils, limited only by federal (not state) law. The Na 'Ohana O Hawaii is one native Hawaiian group, headed by Peggy Ha'o Ross, who claims that Hawaii was overthrown illegally and should still be ruled by descendants of Hawaiian royalty. Ross herself claims to be heir to the throne by descent. The group issued a Declaration of Independence from the U. S. in 1980. Followers list their national affiliation as members of the Native Hawaiian Nation.

Let's turn to economic aspects of the question. Under state law, persons of Hawaiian descent have rights to lands or land revenues once belonging to the crown. To qualify for these rights, a person must prove that he or she possesses at least 50 percent blood quantum, or 50 percent Hawaiian blood. The Hawaiian Homes Act in 1921 declared that a portion of the income from crown lands (lands belonging to the royal family and ceded to the state when Hawaii entered the Union) would be used to benefit Hawaiians. Because so many Hawaiians have married those of other backgrounds, and continue to do so, the number of those qualifying is on the decline. At present, about 70,000 persons of Hawaiian or part-Hawaiian descent qualify for these benefits; but, by the middle of the next century, only half that number will. An additional knotty problem occurs in dispensing these funds. Currently, most of them go into general accounts of the state to be used for items such as transportation and education—items that benefit everyone, but not specifically Hawaiians in the way the Act seemed to intend. Finally, Hawaiians of sufficient blood quantum are eligible under the same Hawaiian Homes Act for parcels of land (see **Hawaiian Homesteads**).

Socially, to be a native Hawaiian can mean many things. It can mean inheriting a pride in one's family and traditions and an awareness of the gifts that the Hawaiian people continue to give: the *aloha* feeling, the heritage of dance and song, a closeness to family and to the land. It also means being aware that one's race almost died off because of diseases brought in from the outside; that distressing levels of economic, educational, and social problems afflict one's people; and that even as the Hawaiian people share their gifts, the vital core of their heritage—the language and oral traditions—survive less and less as living things.

NENE

This Hawaiian goose (*Branta sandvicensis*), a relative of the Canada goose, is the state bird, a fact which has naturally focused special attention on efforts to bring it back from near extinction. It descends from geese that migrated to Hawaii thousands of years ago and eventually lost both their migratory instincts and their adaptation to water habitats. The nene now lives on grassy lava slopes of Mauna Kea and Mauna Loa on the Big Island and Haleakala crater on Maui.

Hunters and animal predators nearly put an end to the species by the early 1900s. In 1940, only a few dozen birds could be counted living wild. To bring them back, they were grown in captivity in England and then reintroduced on Maui and the Big Island, where they are making a slow comeback.

NIGHT MARCHERS

The spirits of Hawaiian warriors are said to march at night on trails leading from inland areas to the sea. People who claim to have witnessed them (there are many) say their warning shouts and drums can be heard before they draw near, and that it is best to hide off the trail when they pass, since they may kill anyone in their way. Their marching is often taken as a sign that someone in the vicinity or family will soon die.

NINE-COURSE DINNER

The Chinese nine-course dinner is served on weddings, important birthdays, and other special occasions, usually in a restaurant or hotel.

The dinner has no fixed menu. On the contrary, the host and cook may stress originality in new dishes and delicate seasonings. The number nine and the plenitude of food have symbolic meaning. Nine connotes height and age, and the bounty of food connotes prosperity.

A typical course of dishes described by one restaurant manager is as follows: 1. Soup 2. Chicken 3. Duck 4. Oysters 5. Sea food 6. Sweet pork or fish 7. Abalone and mushrooms 8. Roast red pork 9. Noodles. Many of these dishes have symbolic meanings. For example, the red coloring and the fat in roast pork stand for prosperity.

OHANA

'Ohana is the extended family. This term carries deep meaning for those of Hawaiian descent, a meaning that has intensified in some ways as the values of the old *'ohana* system are reapplied in new situations.

The *'ohana* is not only the extended family, but the way the Hawaiian family lives and works together. Until recently, many extended families (including grandparents, aunts, uncles, and cousins) lived together or in close proximity. They shared in working, playing, teaching children, and resolving problems. Because of this togetherness, family members developed strong group loyalty and a sense of belonging. Everyone felt responsible to avoid shaming the family. The bond between grandparents and children was especially strong because the elderly did much of the work of caring for children and teaching them proper habits and attitudes. Elders also held great sway in ordering family affairs, giving counsel, and resolving family differences. Even today, when most families live apart from their relations, elder members have a respected position in coordinating family matters.

In the *'ohana* system, marriage ties to other families become spiritual as well. Each *'ohana* has its family gods or ***aumakua***, which have to be respected by both families.

Problems that occur in the extended family are resolved through *ho'oponopono*, a family meeting in which differences are expressed honestly but sensitively and then solutions are found. Solutions often require forgiveness and compromise, important values of the *'ohana.* In summary, the *'ohana* emphasizes sharing, loyalty, respect, unselfishness, and responsibility.

In the last few decades, the term *'ohana* has taken on political overtones. Groups such as the Protect Kahoolawe 'Ohana have made use of the *'ohana* concept to bring a sense of unity and loyalty to their groups and purposes. Other groups such as *hula halau* stress *'ohana* as a way of bringing closeness and commitment among members. Some people question this use of the term, since one cannot make the blood relations that are essential to the *'ohana;* others see the use as a legitimate way of keeping old values alive in new situations. Concerning the latter usage, several authorities have observed that "if we want to stay within the bounds of traditional definition, it's stretching the *'ohana* concept pretty far. What is most often meant are the characteristics of the *'ohana*, such as cooperation and feelings of cohesiveness and unity."(19)

OKOLEHAO

A liquor made from the root of the *ti* plant. *Okolehao* literally means "iron bottom," in reference to the metal stills and blubber pots in which the beverage was brewed and distilled. *Okolehao* is a home brew and is not sold in bars, so don't ask the bartender for a shot.

OLI • Hawaiian for chant.

PAKE

Pake is the local term for Chinese. There is no conclusive account of where the term comes from, though some have asserted it derives from the Chinese word *pak*, for uncle.

PALAKA

Want to really declare your *kama'aina* status? Wear a *palaka* shirt.

Palaka refers to a blue and white checkered cloth favored by plantation workers because of its combination of color and light weight. *Palaka* shirts were cool enough to wear in the tropical heat, sturdy enough to last and give protection from fieldwork, and decorative.

The term *palaka* seems to have derived from the Hawaiian pronunciation of *block* (i.e., checkered) or *frock* and originally applied to any work shirt, but by the turn of the century it named only the checkered cloth and shirts made from it.

PANIOLO • Hawaiian-style cowboy.

The first cattle handlers in Hawaii were Spanish-Mexican *vaqueros* who came in 1832 at the request of King Kamehameha III to teach Islanders how to range the cattle that had been introduced by Captain George Vancouver of Great Britain in 1793. Islanders adapted their word of self-description, *Espanol,* into a more easily pronounced *paniolo.* These colorful *vaqueros* soon engaged the leisurely Hawaiians with their enthusiasm, dedication, and cattle-handling abilities. Just as Hawaii produced its own term for cowboy from the languages used by Spanish-American cow punchers, it also created its own breed of cowboy from the merging of island traits and the imported culture of cattle ranching. Today the great cattle ranches of Hawaii (one of the largest privately owned ranches in the world, the Parker Ranch, is located on the Big Island) still function with the *paniolo* in the saddle. The bright wool ponchos, slashed leggings, bandannas, and wide sombreros of the original *vaqueros* have given way to jeans, *palaka* prints or T-shirts, leather jackets, and boots. However, the cowboy hat, often adorned with a *lei* of flowers or shells, is symbolic of the successful combination of the rugged courage, expertise, and dedication of the *vaquero* with the contagious Hawaiian *aloha* spirit and native charm found in the *paniolo.*

The book *Paniolo* describes the Hawaiian cowboy this way: He's a hard riding man, leather-tough—a laughing man—and often with a lei of pansies around the crown of his hat. He has what the Hawaiians call *manao*—the spirit and feel of the true Hawaiian. Some say he is a lonely man; lonely because he rides alone so much. Maybe the quiet hills and plateaus bring on that quality. We see the *paniolo* as a person with the quiet sensitivity of a man who has lived for a long time with his loneliness and who is now on good terms with it. He's a man who understands the whispered language of nature. He is also a quality cowboy.(20)

PA'U RIDER

A distinctive and beautiful feature of parades in Hawaii, the *pa'u* rider is a woman on horseback wearing a long, split gown or skirt that hangs over each side of the horse. In major parades, such as that of Kamehameha Day in June, *pa'u* riders represent each island of the State of Hawaii. The *pa'u* unit for each island may consist of up to seven people: a princess, her attendants, male escorts, and a page. Riders are sometimes the winners of beauty and talent contests, but often they are selected from among applicants by parade commissions. However chosen, riders consider it an honor to grace the parade and represent the Islands.

The *pa'u* is the dress itself, which evolved from a long wrap-around of a single piece of cloth which island women wore while riding horses. The side-saddle position popular among women of Europe and North America never caught on among Hawaii's women. They preferred to straddle a horse, but this position had several disadvantages. First was the problem of modesty, and, second, the problem of protecting dresses from brush and snags. The long wrap-around of calico solved them both. Today, *pa'u* skirts of calico have given way to finer materials more suitable for the pageantry of parades. They are usually made of satin or velvet in the official colors of each island: red for Hawaii, pink for Maui, orange for Lanai, gray for Kahoolawe, green for Molokai, gold for Oahu, purple for Kauai, and brown for Niihau.

PELE'S HAIR

Pele was (is) the goddess of fire and volcanos. The fine, glassy strands of lava formed when drops of lava fall through the air are named for her—Pele's hair.

PICTURE BRIDE

Most immigrant workers recruited for plantations in the late 1800s and early 1900s were single, poor males who came to Hawaii to escape conditions in the homeland. Most planned to return to their native countries after saving enough money. Those who stayed in Hawaii had almost no prospects of marrying within their nationality unless they left a woman they could send for or had family who could arrange such matters. Those with strong cultural norms to marry only their own kind, such as the Japanese, had one remaining alternative—to select a young woman from a photograph sent by family members or marriage brokers. From the years 1908 to 1915, fifty-eight percent of Japanese women arriving in Hawaii were picture brides.

Naturally, this was a risky process. One can imagine the kinds of expectations a man or a prospective bride could form from a photograph. In *Japanese Women in Hawaii*, the recollections of a Japanese man going to meet his bride at Honolulu harbor are recorded:

> Picture brides were often disappointed in the man they came to marry .... There were ten of us who went to pick up our ten brides. . . . My wife and I had already been married two years by having her registered in our family records back in Japan. She was the niece of my friend who had returned to Japan earlier. I asked him to look around for a wife for me and he said he thought his niece was best. He sent me her picture, so I knew what she looked like. Oh, she was the prettiest of all the girls there; she was even prettier than her picture. My heart just pounded with joy because I was so proud of her. She didn't look disappointed when she saw me, and I was happy about that too.
>
> Some picture brides wanted to go back to Japan—they didn't like the looks of Hawaii and of the men they had married. But Mr. Katsunuma, the immigration inspector, told them, "Look, since you're in Hawaii, why don't you stay for a while? If you absolutely don't want to stay, then you can go back later. Or you might find another man, because there are lots of single men here."(21)

Immigration officials, in fact, were often suspicious of picture brides. They were not acquainted with the tradition of arranged marriages and believed that many women arriving as brides were lewd and undesirable. The practice was banned in 1924 by the Oriental Exclusion Act.

PIDGIN

Wassamattah you? Cannah talk da kine? (What's the matter? Can't you speak pidgin?)

Pidgin, as you no doubt will find out soon after arriving, is the local language—not so much of big business or public affairs, but of everyday give and take among the Hawaii born. Its colorful phrasing and intonation are as much a part of the local landscape as plumeria trees and curling waves. You may react to it with distate or delight. Before your reactions harden and you decide just how much of the local lingo you're going to master, consider the following viewpoints of long-time residents.

Knowing a few phrases will help you understand and fit into the flow of life in Hawaii. You'll capsize from time to time without it. But don't feel you need to master pidgin in order to get along. In trying to use it without knowing it inside out, you may create as much embarrassment as anything. Most locals are proud of the power of pidgin. It is an attractive, distinctive cultural statement, but they don't see why newcomers need to sound like them. In fact, a *haole's* imitation of local intonation and lingo can seem patronizing and phony. So be yourself. Talk your own language, but know enough words and phrases to help you understand others and communicate clearly. How much you will need will depend on where you work and what neighborhood you live in.

If you have children, they will most likely come home from school or play speaking a little pidgin. Don't insist on correct English out of fear that their language is going to pot. They are just learning to fit in with their playmates and are fully capable of learning and using one language among friends and another at home. Most children's language abilities are not restricted by their use of pidgin. On the contrary, their familiarity with it is linguistic enrichment.

Some language purists view pidgin as an inferior, broken English, but this is not so. What we call pidgin, linguists call Hawaiian Creole English. Linguists do use the term "pidgin" to refer to a simplified, incomplete version of another language, but that is not what we have in Hawaii. A true pidgin can result when immigrants of various language backgrounds must communicate with each other and so adopt a broken version of a common language, such as the language of the bosses. A pidgin, in this sense, was spoken by many first-generation immigrants who worked Hawaii's sugar and pineapple plantations. A creole language, on the other hand, is similar to a dominant language on which it is patterned but has its own unique vocabulary and syntax. In other words, it is a language in its own right.

Pidgin grew out of the need to communicate among immigrant labor forces and plantation overseers. At first, the common medium of communication was built out of a small vocabulary of English and Hawaiian with the barest minimum of grammar. First-generation immigrants often have retained this kind of pidgin throughout their lives and still speak it when they can't talk their native language. Their children fashioned Hawaiian Creole English—what we now usually call pidgin. Since children of immigrants often attended school with children of other language backgrounds, and sometimes came from homes in which parents spoke different languages, their natural language-learning abilities molded a language based on English but with some rules of its own. Linguists have found that Hawaiian Creole English has features found in other creole languages arising in similar circumstances. This fact has made our pidgin a topic of study because linguists believe that it reveals certain universals about how humans create and use language.

Pidgin has helped maintain the local sense of difference and identity. Proficiency carries the message: "I'm on my own turf, among my own kind." Whereas pidgin was considered low class for decades after it arose, it is now frequently used in politics and negotiations. A local business leader and labor negotiator commented on how pidgin can break the white boss/local laborer barrier:

> You use it to make a point. Like when we're in union negotiations. At those meetings you don't want to come across as the

> BIG WHITE BWANA talking to the local spearchuckers. They (the union negotiators) tend not to be as tense if you can come across as another local guy who can say, "I was born and raised here, like you."(22)

You can hardly miss picking up a basic vocabulary of pidgin (almost everyone uses a little, and it frequently appears in advertising), but you might not pick out some of the verbs and structures that govern pidgin sentences. So here is a comparison between English and pidgin. Note that "wen" or "bin" is used often to create past tense for verbs, "stay" for present or progressive (ongoing) time, and "go" for future.

English	**Pidgin/ Hawaiian Creole English**
The two of us had a hard time raising dogs.	Us two bin get hard time raising dog.
John and his friends are stealing the food.	John-them stay cockaroach the kaukau.
He doesn't want to play because he's lazy.	He lazy, 'a'swhy he no like play.
How do you expect to finish your house?	How you expect for make pau you house?
It would have been better if I'd gone to Honolulu to buy it.	More better I bin go Honolulu for buy om.
The man who was going to lay the vinyl had quoted me the price.	The guy gon' lay the vinyl bin quote me price.
There was a woman who had three daughters.	Bin get one wahine she get three daughter.
She can't go because she hasn't any money.	She no can go, she no more money, 'a'swhy.(23)

Pidgin has long been a political and educational issue. Some residents remember teachers who used little else, but a few years ago the State Department of Education prohibited the use of pidgin as a medium of instruction in schools. This action was hotly debated. One side argued that pidgin, as a fact of life and important part of local culture, deserved to be recognized in the curriculum. The other contended that schools must prepare students to compete for jobs that required command of standard English and that, by communicating in pidgin and spending time discussing it, teachers were dooming students to second-class social and economic lives.

To savor the humor and social nuances of pidgin, browse through Peppo's *Pidgin to da Max*. For a more systematic treatment of the history and characteristics of pidgin, read Elizabeth Carr's *Da Kine Talk*.

Pidgin You Should Know can be found in the **Glossaries** near the end of the book.

PIG HUNTING

If you like to hunt and aren't a bit squeamish about going after game with just about anything available—knives, dogs, magnum pistols, or rifles—and if you get invited to hunt pigs, don't miss the chance. You'll experience the macho side of local life in a way it is rarely seen outside of a good bar fight.

Pigs can be hunted on any island, including Oahu.

Some assume that these pigs are the breed that came to the Islands with Polynesian voyagers, but this is not so. That was a more domesticated variety. The prey of hunters is the feral pig, an acutely intelligent animal (smarter than the dogs used to hunt it, some say) which descends from boars brought to Hawaii by the British in the late 1700s.

Pigs can be hunted in a variety of ways. The most risk-hardy hunt only with dogs and knives. The dogs find, corner, and hold the pig at bay while the hunter moves in for the kill. "Tracker" dogs pick up the scent and lead the pack, "grabbers" take a bitehold, and "helpers" snap and worry the pig without getting a bitehold. To kill the pig, the hunter has to grab the pig by the leg, or somewhere else away from the sharp tusks, and stab it or slit its throat. Many a dog has his last day facing a feral pig. Slightly less risky than knife hunting is pistol packing—preferably with a large caliber revolver. A .357 magnum is about the smallest round hunters use to guarantee a quick kill. Those who hunt with rifles like a quick-pointing, brush-busting weapon such as the .30-30 lever action or a fast-firing, semi-automatic rifle such as the Ruger Mini-14. High-powered loads, such as the .270 or .30-06, are considered too heavy for close-in hunting. They can pass clean through a pig (most weigh between 60 or 70 pounds) and hit a dog.

Some people mistakenly view pig hunters as a threat to wildlife, when in fact botanists agree that the feral pig poses a serious threat to an entire native ecosystem that can never be recovered—Hawaii's rain forests. The pigs destroy the ecosystem by eating plants, stripping bark, and digging up the delicate top layer of forest soil in search of food. By gnawing at the stem of the native *hapu'u* tree fern to get at its starchy core, pigs destroy part of the secondary canopy that helps to shield the other plants from direct sun and weather and regulates humidity in the forest. Since the rare plants of Hawaii's rain forests never evolved means like thorns or thick bark to protect themselves from such animals, they are vulnerable to the disturbance posed by feral pigs. Additionally, mosquitoes that breed in the mud wallows left by pigs are a threat to native birds that have little immunity to insect-borne diseases. Some experts pose a simple choice: destroy the pigs or lose the remaining rain forests.

POLITICAL CAMPAIGNS • See **SIGN WAVING.**

PORDAGEE MOUT

A motor mouth. A person with a Pordagee mout talks incessantly. The term apparently derives from the proverbial ability of Portuguese immigrants to verbalize about almost anything.

PRIMO BEER

Loyal sons of Hawaii—and not a few daughters—would prefer a locally produced beer to anything brewed on the mainland, and until a few years ago, they had their wish in Primo Beer. Primo was brewed beginning in 1896 by the Honolulu Brewing and Malting Co. in a building still standing on Queen Street in Kakaako. After the repeal of prohibition in 1933, a new group founded the Honolulu Brewing Co. on Kapiolani Blvd. and acquired rights to the Primo label. In 1967 the operation was bought out by Schlitz and moved to Pearl City, but the economies of brewing could not justify the investment, so in 1977 Schlitz moved out but continued to brew Primo in Los Angeles. The move left local Primo fans thirsty for its familiar, but distinctive, taste. When Stroh bought Schlitz, it acquired the Primo brand. Since 1986, Stroh has taken a greater interest in Primo and reformulated the brewing recipe.

In its heyday, Primo controlled about sixty percent of the beer market in Hawaii. Today, it has only about a one percent share. But it appears that, with its new formula and corporate interest, it may be making a comeback—a very unusual feat in the brewing industry.

QUILTS

Hawaiian quiltmaking brings together imported techniques with the Hawaiian feel for natural surroundings. Missionary wives first introduced sewing skills, intent on making Hawaiian women into tidy seamstresses. As the use of imported cloth rose and the production of *kapa* declined (*kapa* is the cloth made from beaten bark of the mulberry), Hawaiian women naturally transferred to quilting the floral and geometric designs commonly used on native cloth.

Early quilters tended to employ variations on the "snowflake" design, made by folding and cutting paper, then unfolding the paper and stitching the pattern. More recent quilters have created graceful floral patterns, depicted events in the personal lives of those who made them, or portrayed historical events such as the statehood of Hawaii.

Most museums in Hawaii have collections of quilts, from early to more contemporary. The Bishop Museum is noted for having the finest. It also sponsors classes in quiltmaking.

SALOON PILOT

The saloon pilot or pilot bread is a large cracker, roughly like the American soda cracker, but larger and harder. It descends from ships biscuits used on long voyages which was known as "hardtack." It is made of simple ingredients—flour and a minimum of salt and water—and baked till it is hard and dry. The name "pilot bread" may come from the better sort of biscuits served to a ship's officers.

The bland taste of the saloon pilot makes it ideal for eating with more flavorful foods such as jam, luncheon meat, and Spam.

SHAKA

"Hang loose, Brah!" is the message in this unique local word and gesture. The sign is made by extending the thumb and little finger while curling the middle three fingers into the palm, then giving the hand a twist from the wrist or elbow.

Stories tracing the origins of the shaka sign differ, often depending on the teller's place of growing up. Some windward Oahu residents say it began with Hamana Kalili, who worked at the Kahuku sugar plantation and lost three fingers. As a guard on the plantation train in the 1930s and 40s, Kalili would use his disabled hand to wave off local youth trying to sneak cane from the slow train. The youths in turn used the gesture to warn each other when Kalili was around. The gesture eventually became a greeting among friends. The Kahuku High School football team is said to have adopted it as a pep signal when breaking from the huddle, and from there it spread.

Other locales have different versions. In the Liliha area of Honolulu, people remember a young boy who used the sign to imitate his father, who had lost the middle three fingers. From that origin, it became a neighborhood greeting. Others remember it as a greeting among poor beach people. On Molokai, it was first seen as a signal among members of a motorcycle group.

SHAVE ICE

Unlike the snow cone, which is made of ice crushed into small particles, shave ice is literally shaved or scraped off a block of ice so it has a finer texture. Shave ice is enjoyed not only with fruit-flavored syrups (try the rainbow special with stawberry, lemon, and pineapple or the Hawaiian delight with coconut, pineapple, and banana), but with unusual additions such as vanilla ice cream or sweet-flavored *azuki* beans. Connoisseurs favor shops with "cotton" shave ice—ice that is cloud soft—and homemade syrups, not too sweet.

Just when shave ice first appeared in Hawaii is not clear, but it was apparently introduced by Japanese sugar plantation workers who planed ice shavings from blocks when they gathered on days off. Later, handcranked machines were imported. When the Japanese began moving off the plantations, some set up stores and sold shave ice to the general population.

A favorite shave-ice stop on Oahu, Matsumoto's in Haleiwa, goes through 22,000 pounds of block ice per month during the summer.

SHINTO THANKSGIVING FESTIVAL

This ancient Shinto observance is celebrated on a Sunday in October at the Daijingu Temple. Its meaning has been described in these terms:

> This Shinto festival is closely associated with the rice harvest in Japan. Essentially a thanksgiving celebration of the earth's bounty, it expresses gratitude to the *kami* or living spirit which in Shinto belief joins those who have gone before with those who are still in this world. In this respect it can be considered the Shinto counterpart of the Buddhist Bon Festival.(24)

The celebration includes prayers and purification rituals, offerings, speeches, an outdoor procession with a portable altar known as *mikoshi,* dances by figures representing deities and spirits, and the drinking of *sake.*

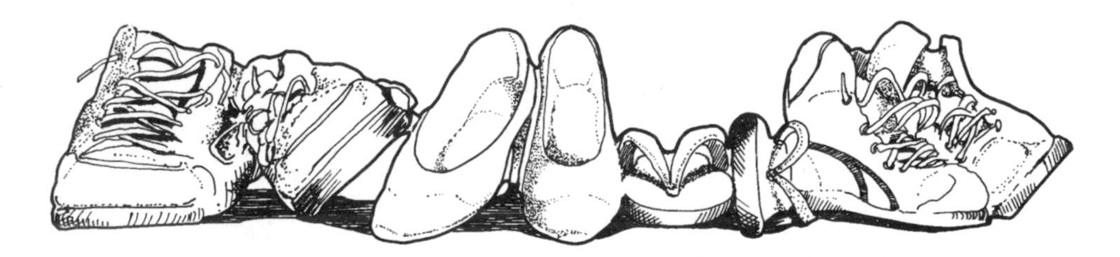

SHOES

You've probably already noticed that people remove their shoes or footwear when entering someone's home. This tradition was brought by the Japanese from their homeland, where it is still everyday protocol.

The removal of shoes has its practical side: leaving shoes at the door makes housekeeping easier, since it keeps dirt and moisture from following one into the house. But it also has its symbolic side. Guests remove their shoes as a sign of respect when entering someone else's home. Additionally, removing one's shoes (the most soiled article of clothing) when entering the home is a way of marking the transition from the outer world with its dirt (both literal and figurative) to the reverence of the family dwelling.

The removing of shoes probably spread beyond the Japanese to become a state-wide tradition because the Hawaiians found it congenial. Hawaiians didn't wear shoes, of course, but they were conscious of their feet in entering a dwelling, even though it might have a dirt floor. They didn't want to bring dirt or unfriendly spirits inside.

SIGN-WAVING CAMPAIGNS

At election time you'll find the roads lined with people waving signs and waving at you as you drive by . Surely, you may say, this is one of the most labor-intensive campaign methods ever invented. It is also one of the established practices of Hawaii politics.

One political historian locates the beginning of roadside waving to the election campaigns in Manoa Valley during 1964 and 1966. By the 70s the practice had spread to all the islands and had become something of a fixture of local electioneering. Not that every candidate sends backers out on the highways during morning and evening rush hours; some consider sign waving merely an amusing distraction with little serious content.

Why does sign waving continue when it requires enormous human effort and organization? After all, those people you see actually got out of bed or left work early to hold those signs. A small part of the answer is that Hawaii does not allow highway billboard advertising. More important, what you're seeing is the Hawaii "people touch" in action. It's not just the sign that advertises. There are other ways of getting a candidate's name before the public. The people who stand there show that the candidate has real people committed to his or her cause. Standing by the side of the road exposes the candidate and his or her supporters to people in a way television advertisements and pamphlets do not. So next election time, enjoy the custom. Wave back.

SLACK-KEY GUITAR

The unusual harmonic sound of this island style of guitar playing comes from its tuning, called "slack key." In standard guitar tuning, each string is tuned to a different note: E A D G B E is nearly universal. When the guitar is strummed without fingering, one gets a sour, unharmonic mix of sounds. In slack key, the strings are tuned to a chord so they harmonize even without fingering.

Slack key is reported to have originated when the Hawaiian ***paniolos***, musically inclined but unable to read or write musical scores, tried to master the guitar and found little sense in an arrangement of strings that jar when strummed together. They invented other tunings by loosening or slackening strings to produce chords matched to the singer's vocal range or to the songs being sung. In the most common slack-key tuning, the G or "*taro*-patch" tuning, the strings are tuned D G D G B D. The *"wahine"* tuning contains the notes D A D F# A C#. Another common tuning, the A tuning, contains only two notes: E A E E A E. Beyond these, the variety is practically limitless. In any tuning, the repetition of a base note with harmonic notes building above it gives the guitar greater richness of sound within a few notes of the chord.

In playing standard guitar, the musician generally strums chords or picks notes. In playing slack key, the musician may pluck the melody on the higher strings while accompanying it with the tuned base strings. The twang sounds one hears in slack key are the overtones or "harmonics" that result when the strings are fingered on the twelfth fret.

SLIPPERS

Elsewhere, one might call these *zoris* or thongs or flip-flops. In Hawaii they are slippers—or, more correctly, slippahs.

STATE ANTHEM • See **HAWAII PONO'I.**

STATE BIRD • See **NENE.**

STATE FLAG

You may wonder why Hawaii's state flag looks like a combination of the British Union Jack and the Stars and Stripes. The answer: that's exactly what it is. The eight stripes of white, red, and blue are easy to explain. They represent the eight major islands and echo the red and white stripes of the United States flag. But why the Union Jack?

British sailors discovered Hawaii and played a significant role in helping it maintain its sovereignty. In 1794 Captain George Vancouver helped King Kamehameha I to place Hawaii under British protection. In 1843 the British temporarily gained rule of the Islands by coercing the government of King Kamehameha III into signing an act of provisional cession that placed the government under British control. Actually, the British government did not sanction the takeover, which was carried out by overzealous functionaries when the rights of a British citizen were threatened. If the episode smacks of colonial overkill, it does reveal the tenuous nature of politics and independence in the Kingdom of Hawaii. During the five months the British were legally at the helm, the Hawaiian flag was lowered, and the Union Jack raised. When the British foreign office received a full account of the affair, it disavowed any support, then joined with the U.S. and France to reaffirm the independence of the Islands. So, in spite of the disreputable takeover of 1843, the people of Hawaii memorialized in their state flag their admiration of British people and political traditions.

STATE FLOWER

The state flower is the hibiscus, which grows in thousands of varieties.

STATE MOTTO

The phrase, *"Ua mau ke ea o ka aina i ka pono"* was made the state motto in 1959. King Kamehameha III had struck the Old Testament-sounding phrase in a speech commemorating the restoration of sovereignty after a brief period during which the British had assumed rule of the Islands. Translated, it means "The life of the land is perpetuated in righteousness."

STATE TREE • See **KUKUI**.

STINK EYE • A dirty look.

STREET NAMES

Where else but in Hawaii? A special committee makes sure that new street names are rendered in correct Hawaiian and contain no unwanted double meanings. New street names on Oahu are chosen by developers but must then pass the scrutiny of this committee, part of the City and County Department of Land Utilization. Recent developers have tended to select street names by topic or theme: heavenly bodies, sea creatures, flowers and plants, etc.

SURFING

If you want to try this authentic Hawaiian sport and have no experience, go to Waikiki with a friend and rent a long "tanker" board from one of the beach rental stands in front of the major hotels or near the public restrooms just Diamond Head of the Moana Hotel. When you have your board, look around for the places where surfing instructors wait with their customers for small waves and take your place near them. Your friend is along so you can take turns holding the board steady and giving the forward shove needed to start you on a beginner's wave.

Surfers are generally laid back and tanned, but there is no true stereotype. What they share is their love of surfing, an experience they know in their feet, legs, and pits of their stomachs. When they take on the big waves, they match human strength, balance, wits, and courage against crushing power loosed in the curl of awesome breakers. The experience of floating offshore, sometimes for hours, waiting for good sets of waves and reading the swells, makes them keenly observant of ocean conditions. They tend to be environmentally minded. They know the beauty of pristine beach and clear water.

Surfers often have to answer the question: How do you support yourselves? Some hold 9-to-5 jobs and surf early or late in the day and on weekends. A small number are sponsored by surfing equipment manufacturers or live on endorsements and prize money from the big competitions. Others seem to enjoy financial independence, and another set works the welfare, unemployment, and food stamp system.

Surfing competitions come during December and January (the

months of heavy surf) on the North Shore at Sunset, Pipeline, and Waimea. The keenest international competitors arrive for three meets that together make up the Corona Triple Crown: the World Cup of Surfing, the Pipeline Masters, and the Billabong Pro. Prize money runs from $35,000 to $100,000 for each meet.

SUMO WRESTLING

Sumo is a Japanese form of belt wrestling in which specially trained athletes compete to throw each other out of a ring. Nearly every aspect of the sport is governed by ritual: the top-knot hair, the long silk band and hanging strands of the belt, the salt thrown to purify the ring, and so forth.

The first Japanese immigrants brought *sumo* with them. The first recorded *sumo* match came in 1885; King Kalakaua attended to celebrate the arrival of more Japanese laborers. *Sumo* has grown in appeal in modern Hawaii as promoters have brought in *sumo* competitions, but local people have also taken a special interest in the sport since a Maui man of Hawaiian ancestry became the first non-Japanese to be accepted by a *sumo* master as part of his "stable" of wrestlers and to compete successfully. This man is Jesse "Takamiyama" Kuhaulua, who in 1972 was awarded the Emperor's Cup, a highly prized recognition. Hawaii has since produced several other notable *sumo* wrestlers. The local Samoan Salevaa Atisanoe, a 500-pound giant from the leeward side of Oahu, wrestles under the name "Konishiki." Another rising star is the former Waianae High School wrestler and football player Chad Rowan, who weighs in at over 400 pounds and wrestles under the name "Akebono."

TALK STINK

On the mainland, you badmouth someone; you cut them down. In Hawaii you talk stink.

TALK STORY

To talk story means to converse casually, to tell stories one to another, to shoot the breeze. Beyond that, to talk story is to allow lives to make contact through the medium of words. It is taking time to tell and listen without having a set objective, sharing experiences recent or remote as they are called up by memory and association. As one person expressed it: "Talking story is more than just the story. The same incidents may come up several times. As we go over them, and as the feelings bounce around from one person to another, we get their meaning down. It involves what we say and the way we say it and how it feels with us in it, as part of it."

TITA

A *tita* is young woman. The term has two connotations. It may refer to the rough-and-tough, belligerent kind, or it may be used as a term of endearment, like "sister."

TSUNAMI

Tsunami means "storm wave" in Japanese. Some people erroneously call this a "tidal wave," but it has nothing to do with tides. Created by the shock of an earthquake, a *tsunami* can travel up to 500 miles an hour for thousands of miles as a barely observable swell. When it approaches shallower water near land, however, it slows down while it gains height, then unleashes its enormous fury on exposed coastal areas.

Although a few *tsunamis* have been caused by quakes in the Islands, the most destructive ones have usually come from quakes along South American coasts or in the extreme North Pacific. The most destructive *tsunamis* of recent decades hit Hawaii in 1946 and 1960 (159 deaths and over $26 million in damage in 1946). Numerous smaller waves have passed through causing moderate or no damage. Because they can be predicted only after an earthquake has happened, Hawaii has a *tsunami* warning system on all populated islands. The warning sirens are yellow cannister-like objects about the size of small garbage cans mounted on utility poles along the shore highways. These are tested at regular intervals, so you'll get to know what they sound like if you live in an exposed area. The opening section of your telephone book has maps showing which areas can anticipate flooding.

UKULELE

"My dog has fleas." These words, often sung to the notes to which the *ukulele* is tuned, have more than a casual application to the instrument. The terms *`uku* or flea and *lele* or hop together mean "jumping flea," an apt description of the quick strumming action with which the *ukulele* is played.

The *ukulele* is a small, four-stringed instrument adapted from the small guitar-like instrument, the *machete da braca,* brought to Hawaii by Portuguese immigrants from Madeira in the late 1870s. Here, the instrument caught on because it was less expensive, lighter, and easier to master than the full-sized guitar. Its new, highly descriptive name must also have added to its popularity. Artists such as Arthur Godfrey, who played the *ukulele,* eventually spread its popularity outside Hawaii.

The *ukulele* comes in the standard size (which could be called soprano) as well as tenor and baritone varieties, the latter two larger and lower pitched than the first. The *ukulele* is usually tuned g-c-e-a in Hawaii. Elsewhere, its standard tuning, which matches the guitar tuning, is generally a-d-f#-b.

If you want to buy a *ukulele* that will last for years and hold tune, avoid the cheap ones sold in many tourist shops. They make good souvenirs but not good music. They have poor tone and do not hold on key. Although nearly all the big guitar makers produce good quality instruments, local musicians prize the Kamaka *ukulele,* made of *koa* wood.

UKUPAU

If you ever wished you could leave work when you finished your tasks for the day instead of waiting for the clock to strike, then you already understand the *ukupau* philosophy. Literally, *ukupau* means "finished pay," and it means that you do your job and then enjoy the rest of the day as you want. Hawaii's garbage collectors work under this system, which explains why they run down the street instead of ambling along like mainland sanitation workers.

The *ukupau* attitude can be traced back to ancient Hawaii when clock time did not exist, only work to be performed. Later, some plantations allowed workers to do an expected amount of work no matter how long or short it took. Of course, most workers preferred to work as quickly as possible and reward themselves with extra time off.

Ukupau also carries connotations of pitching in, working together to accomplish something that needs doing.

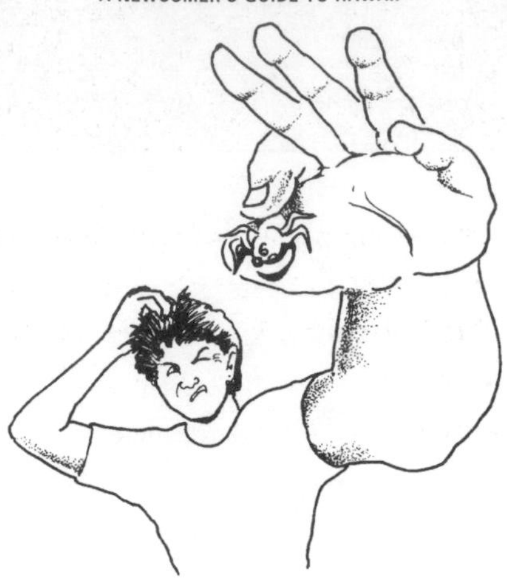

UKUS

When you hear that your child has *ukus*, it means he or she has tiny head lice in the hair. Because of Hawaii's warm climate, head lice breed as if in an incubator. They also spread easily, transferring from one head to another at the slightest contact, so don't be alarmed or upset if your child gets them. It is not a sign that the hygiene of local people is sadly in need of your supervision. School officials conduct periodic checks to determine if children are infested.

Good hygiene goes a long way toward keeping *ukus* away, but given the way children play, it's nearly impossible to prevent *ukus* altogether. Once they cross from one head to another, they begin to lay eggs along hairs. A close examination can reveal the nits, or tiny eggs, as well as the nearly invisible lice that move up and down along single strands of hair.

A druggist can recommend an over-the-counter shampoo like "Nix" to kill *ukus*, or you may ask your doctor to prescribe "Kwell" shampoo or its equivalent. Several applications, following directions, will rid a head of lice. Use caution in applying "Kwell" to children—its active ingredient is a pesticide that can be absorbed through the skin and cause undesirable side effects.

WEDDINGS • See CHINESE WEDDING.

GLOSSARIES

GENERAL AND MISCELLANEOUS TERMS

This general glossary includes non-Hawaiian words that are not featured in the **Alphabetical Guide**. Glossaries of Hawaiian and pidgin follow this general glossary, so if you don't find the term you're looking for here, please check there.

banzai—[Japanese] "hurrah!" shouted at weddings and other occasions. Also, a cheer given when drinking
bento—[Japanese] a combination plate lunch of Japanese foods
chi-chi—[Japanese] breasts
compadre—[Filipino] a member of a group of friends who help each other. A godparent
furo—[Japanese] a hot bath
futon—[Japanese] cushions or thin mattress for sleeping
hibachi—[Japanese] a small, portable charcoal cooker
issei—[Japanese] a first-generation Japanese immigrant
ken—[Japanese] a prefecture or governmental district of Japan
koi nobori—[Japanese] carp flags or streamers displayed on Boys' Day
manong—[Filipino] an older man or older brother. A Filipino
musubi—[Japanese] rice ball
namasu—[Japanese] meat and vegetable dish
nisei—[Japanese] second-generation Japanese, children of issei
saimin—[Chinese or pidgin] noodles
sakada—[Filipino] laborer working away from the homeland
sansei—[Japanese] third-generation Japanese-American
sashimi—[Japanese] raw fish
shoyu—[Japanese] soy sauce
sushi—[Japanese] a food made of vinegar-seasoned rice, fish, and other ingredients
tanomoshi—[Japanese] rotating credit association
won bok—[Chinese] Chinese cabbage
yonsei—[Japanese] fourth-generation Japanese-American

SAY IT IN HAWAIIAN

Pronunciation. The written Hawaiian language has five vowels (a, e, i, o, and u) and seven consonants (h, k, l, m, n, p, and w) as standardized by missionaries in the early 1800s.

Vowels are pronounced

a—ah, as in bar
e—ay, as in plane or eh , as in bet
i—ee, as in keen
o—oh, as in home
u—oo, as in tool

Some vowel combinations (called diphthongs) have distinctive sounds:

ai—y, as in my
ao—ow, as in how
oe—oy, as in toy

The small apostrophe-like mark (') before a vowel signals a glottal stop, such as we use when we say "oh-oh!"

Survival List of Hawaiian Words

'a'a—rough lava
'aina—land
aikane—friend, buddy
akamai—smart, clever
ali'i—nobility, chief
aloha—love, hello, good-bye
auwe—too bad, alas
hale—house
hana—work
haole—white person
hapa—half, part. Hapa haole means half white.
hapai—pregnant
heiau—pre-Christian Hawaiian temple
holoholo—go out
holoku—fancy gown
honi—to kiss
huhu—angry
hui—club, society, union
huki—pull
hula—dance
imu—underground oven
i mua—forward
kahili—royal standard
kahuna—expert craftsman, priest
kai—sea
kama'aina—long-time resident or native-born
kanaka—man
kane—male
kapakahi—crooked
kapu—taboo, forbidden
keiki—child
kokua—help

kona—south, leeward
ko'olau—north, windward
kuleana—parcel of property
lanai—porch, terrace, veranda
lauhala—pandanus tree
laulau—portion of food baked in leaves
lei—flower necklace
limu—underwater vegetation, edible seaweed
lomilomi—massage
lua—toilet, bathroom
lu'au—feast
luna—boss, overseer
mahalo—thank you
mahu—homosexual or transvestite
maika'i—good, beautiful
makai—toward the ocean
malihini—newcomer, stranger
malo—loincloth, short wrap-around
mauka—inland, away from the sea
mauna—mountain
mele—chant, song
menehune—legendary dwarfs
moe—sleep
mu'umu'u—a style of loose dress
nani—beautiful
nui—big, great
'oe—you
'ohana—family, extended family
'okole—buttocks
'okolehao—home-brewed liquor
'ono—delicious
'opala—garbage
opihi—an edible shellfish gathered along the shore
'opu-stomach
pahoehoe—smooth lava
pake—Chinese
palapala—writing
pali—cliff
paniolo—cowboy
pau—finished
pikake—jasmine
pilau—stink, filthy
pilikia—trouble
poi—taro paste
pua'a—pig
puka—hole
pupu—snack, hors d'oeuvres
pupule—insane
taro—a starchy staple food in ancient Hawaii. Grown in wet "taro patches," it produces a large, broad leaf and starchy root which can be steamed and eaten plain or pounded into poi.
ti—a plant with long, green leaves used to serve food, make skirts, wrap offerings, etc.
'ukulele—small guitarlike instrument
wahine—female
wiki or **wikiwiki**—hurry, fast

PIDGIN YOU SHOULD KNOW

an den—and then? what's next? big deal
akamai—smart, clever
brah—brother
buggah—pal or pest, depending on tone of voice
bumbye—by and by, soon
bussum out—share what you have there
cockaroach—steal, sneak
da kine—that thing, anything being referred to
Also, that kind of thing
eh brah—hey pal!
fo' what—why?
fo' real—really? for sure
garans—guaranteed
geev 'um—give 'em the works! Go for it! Give 'em hell!
grind—eat
grinds—food
hana hou—again, encore
Hawaiian time—late, as usual
hele on—get moving; right on!

howzit?—hello, how's it going?
huhu—angry
kaukau—eat, food
kay den—OK then! If you insist.
li' dis; li' dat—like this or like that
like beef?—want to fight?
lolo—numb in the head, crazy
lua—bathroom
moke—tough local dude
ono—delicious
pau—finished
pupus—hors d'oeuvres
shaka—right on!
spark—check out, notice
stink eye—dirty look
talk stink—badmouth someone
tita—easy going girl; tough girl
whaddascoops—what's the scoop? what's going on?

SUGGESTED READING

General

Hopkins, Jerry, and others, *Fax to da Max* (Honolulu: Bess Press, 1985).

McDermott, John F., Jr., Wen-Shing Tseng, and Thomas W. Maertzki, eds., *Peoples and Cultures of Hawaii: A Psychocultural Profile* (Honolulu: Univ. of Hawaii Press, 1980).

Ronck, Ronn, *Ronck's Hawaiian Almanac* (Honolulu: Univ. of Hawaii Press, 1984).

Suggs, Robert C., *The Island Civilizations of Polynesia* (New York: Mentor Books, 1960).

History

Daws, Gavan, *Shoal of Time: A History of the Hawaiian Islands* (New York: Macmillan, 1968).

Fuchs, Lawrence H., *Hawaii Pono: A Social History* (New York: Harcourt, Brace, & World, 1961).

Judd, Gerrit P., *Hawaii: An Informal History* (New York: Collier, 1961).

Hawaiians

Handy, E. S., and Mary Kawena Pukui, *The Polynesian Family System in Ka'u, Hawaii* (Rutland, VT: Charles E. Tuttle, 1972).

Kanahele, George Hu'eu Sanford, *Ku Kanaka—Stand Tall: A Search for Hawaiian Values* (Honolulu: Univ. of Hawaii Press, 1986).

Mitchell, Donald D. Kilolani, *Resource Units in Hawaiian Culture* (Honolulu: Kamehameha Schools Press, 1982).

Hawaiian Language

Pukui, Mary Kawena, Samuel H. Elbert, and Esther T. Mookini, *The Pocket Hawaiian Dictionary, with a Concise Hawaiian Grammar* (Honolulu: Univ. of Hawaii Press, 1975).

Chinese

Chung, May Lee, Dorothy Jim Luke, and Margaret Leong Lau, eds., *Traditions for Living: A Booklet of Chinese Customs and Folk Practices in Hawaii,* 2 vols. (Honolulu: Associated Chinese University Women, 1979 and 1989).

Glick, Clarence E., *Sojourners and Settlers: Chinese Immigrants in Hawaii* (Honolulu: Univ. of Hawaii Press, 1980).

Tom, K. S., *Echoes from Old China: Life, Legends and Lore of the Middle Kingdom* (Honolulu: K. S. Tom, 1989).

Japanese

DeFrancis, John, *Things Japanese in Hawaii* (Honolulu: Univ. of Hawaii Press, 1973).

Hazama, Dorothy and Jane Okamoto Komeiji, *Okage Sama De, The Japanese in Hawaii, 1885-1885* (Honolulu: Bess Press, 1986).

Ogawa, Dennis, *Jan Ken Po, The World of Hawaii's Japanese Americans,* 2nd ed. (Honolulu: Univ. of Hawaii Press, 1978).

Ogawa, Dennis, *Kodomo No Tame Ni, For the Sake of the Children* (Honolulu: Univ. of Hawaii Press, 1978).

Okinawans

Uchinanchu: A History of Okinawans in Hawaii (Honolulu: University of Hawaii Ethnic Studies Oral History Project, 1981).

Koreans

Pai, Margaret K., *The Dreams of Two Yi-min* (Honolulu: Univ. of Hawaii Press, 1989).

Patterson, Wayne, *The Korean Frontier in America: Immigration to Hawaii, 1896-1910* (Honolulu: Univ. of Hawaii Press, 1988).

Filipinos

Alcantara, Ruben R., *Sakada: Filipino Adaptation in Hawaii* (Washington, D.C.: Univ. Press of America, 1981).

Anderson, Robert N., with Richard Coller and Rebecca F. Pestano, *Filipinos in Rural Hawaii* (Honolulu: Univ. of Hawaii Press, 1984).

Teodoro, Luis V., Jr., ed., *Out of this Struggle: The Filipinos in Hawaii* (Honolulu: Univ. of Hawaii Press, 1981).

Caucasians

Whittaker, Elvi, *The Mainland Haole: The White Experience in Hawaii* (New York: Columbia Univ. Press, 1986).

Pidgin

Carr, Elizabeth, *Da Kine Talk: From Pidgin to Standard English in Hawaii* (Honolulu: Univ. of Hawaii Press, 1972).

Simonson, Douglas, and others, *Pidgin to da Max* (Honolulu: Bess Press, 1986).

REFERENCES

(1) Elvi Whittaker, *The Mainland Haole: The White Experience in Hawaii* (New York: Columbia Univ. Press, 1986).

(2) Dennis Ogawa, *Kodomo No Tame Ni: For the Sake of the Children* (Honolulu: Univ. of Hawaii Press, 1978), p. xx.

(3) Robert N. Anderson, , with Richard Coller and Rebecca Pestano, *Filipinos in Rural Hawaii* (Honolulu: Univ. of Hawaii Press, 1984), p. 24.

(4) Brett Uprichard, "Interview with Dr. Emmett Aluli," *Honolulu Magazine* July 1988, pp. 42-51.

(5) John Heckathorn, "Made in Hawaii," *Honolulu Magazine* March 1988, pp. 66-84.

(6) George Hu'eu Sanford Kanahele, *Ku Kanaka—Stand Tall: A Search for Hawaiian Values* (Honolulu: Univ. of Hawaii Press, 1986), p. 84.

(7) Mary Kawena Pukui, E. W. Haertig, and Catherine A. Lee, *Nana I Ke Kumu—Look to the Source* (Honolulu: Queen Lili'uokalani Children's Center, 1972), p. 35.

(8) John DeFrancis, *Things Japanese in Hawaii* (Honolulu: Univ. of Hawaii Press, 1973), pp. 45-61.

(9) DeFrancis, pp. 29-30.

(10) Dr. K.S. Tom , "Traditional Chinese Medicine in Hawaii," in Chung, May Lee, Dorothy Jim Luke, and Margaret Leong Lau, eds., *Traditions for Living* (Honolulu: Associated Chinese University Women, 1979), p. 66-70.

(11) Jannie Luke Thom, "Bridal Tea Ceremony," in Chung, Luke and Lau, eds., p. 27-28.

(12) E. S. Craighill Handy, and Mary Kawena Pukui, *The Polynesian Family System in Ka-'u, Hawai'i* (Rutland, Vermont: Charles E. Tuttle, 1972), p. 83.

(13) DeFrancis, p. 27-28.

(14) Pitzer, Pat, "Contemporary Kahuna," *Honolulu Magazine* November 1984, p. 78.

(15) Gerrit P Judd., *Hawaii: An Informal History* (New York: Collier, 1961), p. 25-26.

(16) Adren J. Bird, and Josephine Puninani Kanakea Bird, *Hawaiian Flower Lei Making* (Honolulu: Univ. of Hawaii Press, 1987), p. 1.

(17) "Newcomer's Guide," *Honolulu Magazine* January 1985.

(18) Robert C. Suggs, *The Island Civilizations of Polynesia* (New York: Mentor, 1960), pp. 150-151.

(19) Pukui, Haertig, and Lee, p. 173.

(20) Joseph Brennan, *Paniolo* (Honolulu: Topgallant, 1978), p. 2.

(21) Patsy Saiki, *Japanese Women in Hawaii: The First One Hundred Years* (Honolulu: Kisaku, 1985), p. 67.

(22) Mike Markrich,"Interview with Kent Bowman," *Honolulu Magazine* October 1978, pp. 42-43.

(23) Derek Bickerton, "Creole Languages," *Scientific American* July 1983, p. 119.

(24) DeFrancis, p. 62.

ALSO CONSULTED

Raenette Gee, "The Fruit of Immortality," in Chung, Luke, and Lau, p. 65.

John Heckathorn, "Can Hawaiian Survive?" *Honolulu Magazine* April 1987, p. 48.

Hu, Elsie Loo Hu, "The Nine Course Dinner," in Chung, Luke and Lau, p. 41.

Herb Kane, "They Called It Bread," *Honolulu Magazine* November 1988, p. 78.

Marilyn Kim, "The Lure of Las Vegas," *Honolulu Magazine* April 1986, p. 53.

Dorothy Jim Luke, "Choosing a Name—Chinese Style," in Chung, Luke, and Lau, pp. 32-34.

Alan T. Moriyama, *Imingaisha: Japanese Emigration Companies and Hawaii* (Honolulu: A. T. Moriyama, 1985).

Dennis Ogawa, *Jan Ken Po: The World of Hawaii's Japanese Americans,* 2nd ed. (Honolulu: Univ. of Hawaii Press, 1978).

"Palaka Power," in *"Newcomer's Guide," Honolulu Magazine* January 1988, p. 9.

Archie Satterfield, "A Stitch in Time: Hawaii's Prized Quilts," *Travel Holiday* January 1987, pp. 12-13.

Cheryl Chee Tsutsumu, "Mochi," *In Paradise* January 1989, pp. 22-25.

James C. F. Wang, *Hawaii State and Local Politics* (Hilo: J. C. F. Wang, 1982).